God and Me! 2

Ages 2-5

LEGACY PRESS®

God and Me! 2

Ages 2-5

Lynn Marie-Ittner Klammer

For my husband Mark and my father Ronald Ittner...
the most special men in my life.

GOD AND ME! 2 FOR AGES 2-5
©2008 by Legacy Press, seventh printing
ISBN 10: 1-58411-054-6
ISBN 13: 978-1-58411-054-5
Legacy reorder #LP46827
Juvenile Nonfiction / Religion / Devotion & Prayer

Legacy Press
P.O. Box 261129
San Diego, CA 92196

Interior Illustrator: Aline Heiser
Cover Illustrator: Phyllis Harris

Unless otherwise noted, Scriptures are from the *Holy Bible: New International Version* (North American Edition), copyright ©1973, 1978, 1984 by the International Bible Society. Used by permission of Zondervan Bible Publishers.

Printed in South Korea

 # Table of Contents

 # Table of Contents

 # Table of Contents

Introduction

As I reflect upon this book of devotions, I'm amazed. What a path of learning this has been! These stories about everyday life with my four children have furthered our quest to grow in our faith. But these aren't just our stories, they're your stories too. As anyone with children will attest, the stories in this book are no different from what we all experience in our lives with children. What's special is the reminder of God's love that endures no matter how simple the story, or how common the experience.

With each enclosed story, you will find a related Bible verse, questions to aid your child's comprehension of the text, and a prayer. Following each devotion, there's a fun activity for you to share with your child as well.

Perhaps the most useful aspect of this book, however, is that the devotions are organized by theme. When my little girl wanted to wear her spring coat on a cold, winter day, I wrote about stubbornness. Bedtime battles became a story on responsibility. Whatever your need, or issue you're dealing with on a given day, you can easily look up that theme and find a devotion to address it.

The enclosed stories are all true, and repeatedly demonstrate the opportunity for spiritual learning in our everyday lives. When my daughter wanted a new pet, it was a chance to discuss how we care for God's creation. When she was frightened by medical tests, we talked about how our faith can comfort and strengthen us. In every situation, there is an opportunity to discuss God's teachings. It is my hope that through my example, you will come to make these connections in your everyday life with children as well.

I Can Be My Best for God

Be Honest

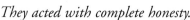

I should be honest.

They acted with complete honesty.

~ 2 Kings 12:15

Who Did It?

"Bobby put sand in my pants!" cried Melissa. Melissa, her sister, Angela, and her cousin Bobby had been playing in the sand box outside.

"Bobby," Aunt Ann asked, "is this true? Did you put sand in Melissa's pants?"

Bobby looked away from Aunt Ann and answered, "No, I didn't. Angela did it."

"He's lying!" screamed Melissa. "He put the sand in my pants!"

Aunt Ann asked him again, "Did you put sand in Melissa's pants?"

Bobby wouldn't look at his aunt as he said, "No, I didn't do it. Angela did it."

"Bobby," said Aunt Ann, "it would be better to admit that you did something bad than to lie and blame someone else for what you did."

Bobby stood very quietly looking down at his feet for a long time. Finally, he admitted that he did put the sand in Melissa's pants.

Aunt Ann was right. Even if you're afraid of being punished, it is still better to be honest about what you did wrong. God wants you to be <u>honest.</u>

Your Turn

1. What did Melissa say that Bobby did?

_____

2. Why do you think Bobby said Angela put the sand in Melissa's pants?

_____

3. Why is it important to be honest and not blame others?

_____

Prayer

God, please forgive me when I do bad things, and help me to remember that I should always be honest. Amen.

Tossing Rings

Read this to your child: "Bobby did something bad, so he felt he had to lie about it to his aunt so he wouldn't get into trouble. If Bobby had played in nice ways instead, he wouldn't have wanted to lie to stay out of trouble. Here's a game that you can play in nice ways. Punch four pencils into a flat piece of cardboard as shown (they do not have to be punched all the way through). Flatten out an empty paper towel tube and cut cross sections from it that are about an inch wide each, then open the pieces out to form rings. Now you're ready to toss the rings at the pencils. How many can you hook onto the pencils?"

Be Smart

I should be smart and sneaky only in good ways.

He will make your paths straight.

~ Proverbs 3:6

Gerbil Getaway

The house was quiet. Everyone was still asleep. Amanda slowly slipped out of her bed and carefully tip-toed across the hall to where her big sister slept. Amanda loved going into Nicole's room, but she wasn't allowed to go in unless she had permission. Amanda knew that if she was very sneaky, she could go in to Nicole's room and back out again before Nicole even knew she was there.

As Amanda walked into Nicole's room, she could feel her heart thumping faster and faster because she was so excited! There were so many pretty toys and fancy dolls that Amanda didn't know where to look first…and then she saw them. Nicole's gerbils had babies, and Amanda couldn't wait to pet their soft, black fur. Soon Amanda had let out all six babies, but then she had a problem. Amanda couldn't catch the gerbils to put them back into the aquarium. Amanda got scared and quickly went back to her room.

When Nicole woke up she realized that her gerbils were out. She was able to catch them all, but the baby gerbils could have been hurt very badly had she not. Amanda was wrong to be sneaky.

God gives you many gifts, like the ability to be smart and sneaky. When you're sneaky to buy someone a surprise gift, that's a good way to be sneaky. But when you use sneakiness to do something bad, God is not happy. God wants you to use what He gives you, even sneakiness, in only good ways.

Your Turn

1. Why did Amanda want to go into Nicole's room even though she knew she wasn't allowed?

   cuss she wh uss not sleepy

2. Have you ever done something sneaky in a good way? In a bad way?

   no

Prayer

Dear God, please help me to only be sneaky in good ways. Amen.

14

Paper Models

Read this to your child: "God wants you to use everything He gives you in good ways, especially your smarts. Here's something you can make as a gift for a friend. Be very smart and sneaky by keeping it a secret until it's done! Wad some old newspapers and soak them in water. Squeeze out the water, and form the newspaper into shapes. Let the shapes dry overnight, then paint your shapes. Here are some of our shapes."

Be Careful

I should think before I act.

Let us be…self-controlled.

~ 1 Thessalonians 5:6

There's a Gerbil in My Hair!

"Help, help," called Morgan from her room upstairs. She sounded scared, but as Mommy saw her run down the stairs, Morgan was smiling.

"What is it?" asked Mommy. "What do you need help with?"

Morgan stood very still as she grinned and said, "Look at my head."

Mommy looked at Morgan's head but didn't see anything. Then suddenly Mommy noticed that Morgan's long, blond hair seemed to be moving at the back of her neck.

"There's a gerbil in my hair!" Morgan exclaimed with glee.

"Oh, Morgan, what have you done?" said Mommy as she saw the small gerbil struggling to get free of Morgan's hair.

"This is very dangerous," Mommy said as she carefully untangled the gerbil. "What if he had fallen while you were walking downstairs? You wouldn't want something bad to happen to your gerbil, would you?"

Morgan hadn't thought about all the bad things that could happen. She just thought it would be fun to have a gerbil in her hair.

God doesn't want you to do things that could cause something bad to happen. Morgan thought it would be fun to put her gerbil in her hair. She didn't take the time to think what might happen as a result of what she did. God wants you to think before you act.

Your Turn

1. What bad things could have happened to Morgan's gerbil?

_____

_____

2. What is something you have done that you should have given more thought before you acted?

_____

_____

Prayer

God, please help me to think before I act. Amen.

16

Morgan's Gerbil

Read this to your child: "God wants you to think before you act so something bad doesn't happen. Morgan didn't think about how her gerbil could get hurt by what she did. God wants you to be careful and safe. Here's a picture of Morgan and her gerbil. Color Morgan to look like you."

Be Thoughtful

I can exaggerate as long as I think everyone will understand.

Guide me in your truth and teach me.

~ Psalm 25:5

Eating Garbage

Maddy loved to go to Grandma Shirley's house. It was one of her favorite things to do. Grandma always let Maddy do whatever she wanted. She could eat in the living room, watch cartoons for a long time, play with toys or video games and have lots of treats. She could even go outside and feed Grandma's kitties. It was lots of fun!

One day when Maddy was visiting her grandma, she had eaten quite a few treats. Grandma wanted Maddy to stop eating for a while, but Maddy wouldn't listen. Finally, Grandma told her, "No more candy, Maddy. You're going home soon, and if you eat any more garbage you won't eat your good food."

Maddy looked up at Grandma and asked, "You've been feeding me garbage?"

Maddy didn't understand that Grandma was calling candy "garbage" not because it really was garbage but because compared to healthy food, candy isn't very good for you. Grandma wasn't lying, she was just exaggerating a little to make a point.

God does not want you to lie, but it is sometimes okay to exaggerate. As long as everyone understands you're exaggerating, it is not lying. Be sure to think before you exaggerate, so you won't confuse others.

Your Turn

1. Why did Grandma call candy "garbage"?

_____

_____

2. Can you think of anything about which you exaggerate?

_____

_____

Prayer

Dear God, I'll try my best to only exaggerate when everyone knows what I'm doing. Amen.

Counting Candy

Read this to your child: "God does not want you to lie, but it's okay to exaggerate sometimes as long as people know that's what you're doing. Maddy loves candy, but she sometimes eats too much. Can you count the pieces of candy that Maddy ate? Draw a line from the candy to the correct number."

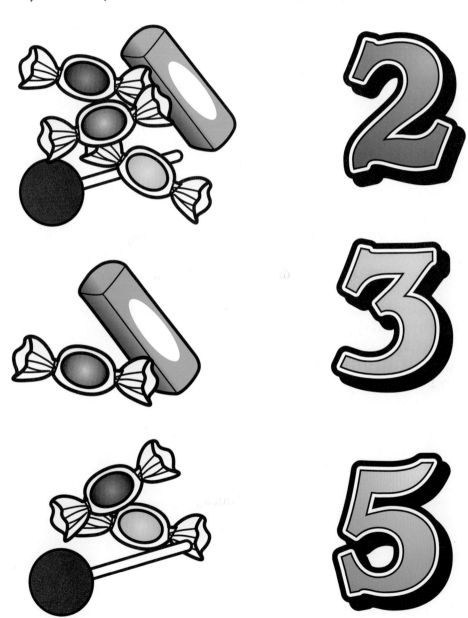

Be Sincere

I should be sincere and not fool others.

An honest answer is like a kiss on the lips.

~ Proverbs 24:26

Lyla's Deception

Lyla climbed up on the chair beside Mommy. She wanted to watch as Mommy put the decorations into their new aquarium. Mommy had told the children that they could each choose a pet, and Lyla and her sister both chose fish. Putting decorations in the aquarium was the last thing they had to do before they put in the fish.

"Don't touch the water," said Mommy, as she lowered her arms into the aquarium. "You can stand there and watch as long as you don't touch. Your hands aren't clean, and I don't want you to get wet either."

Lyla waited until she knew Mommy was busy somewhere else, then she quietly put first one finger and then another into the water.

"I love you," called Lyla as she placed each finger into the water. "I love you, I love you," she said over and over.

Lyla believed that if she said "I love you" again and again, Mommy wouldn't know she was doing something bad. But Lyla was wrong to do what she did. She was trying to fool her mommy so her Mommy wouldn't notice the bad thing she was doing.

God wants you to be sincere, and to not fool other people, especially your mommy and daddy.

Your Turn

1. Did Lyla do something wrong? Why?

_____

_____

2. Tell about a time you tried to fool someone in a bad way.

_____

_____

Prayer

Dear God, I want to be sincere all the time. Please help me not to want to fool other people. Amen.

Castanet Fun

Read this to your child: "God wants you to be sincere and not fool people. Here's something that looks like castanets, but really isn't...but that's okay, using these won't really fool anyone! Castanets are musical instruments that are usually made from wood. People in Spain use them. To make your own toys that are like castanets, glue pieces of string or yarn to four metal lids (found on baby food or olive-size jars). When the glue is dry, slip the loops over your fingers (two on each hand). Now you can make music by clicking together the 'castanets' on each hand."

Be Cooperative

To live God's way, I should cooperate.

They…acknowledged that God's way was right.
~ Luke 7:29

Special Coat

"No!" cried Annabel. "I want to wear this coat!"

Annabel had received a lightweight jacket from her grandma. It was very pretty, with little pink flowers and a tiny house stitched on the front of it. Grandma had given it to her in the spring, but now it was almost winter and the weather was getting much colder. Her light jacket was not warm enough for the cold weather.

"I know you like your jacket, Annabel," Mommy explained, "but it's much too cold now to wear it. You need something warmer."

"No," Annabel insisted. "This is my special coat. Grandma got it for me."

Annabel was not cooperative. She didn't want to wear her winter coat even though she knew her jacket wouldn't keep her warm enough. Mommy knew that Annabel needed her winter coat so she would be warm in the cold weather.

God doesn't want you to be stubborn. He knows that stubbornness can cause you to be hurt or hurt others. To live God's way, be cooperative.

Your Turn

1. Why didn't Annabel want to change to a different coat?

_____

_____

2. What have you done out of stubbornness?

_____

_____

3. Why does God want you to be cooperative?

_____

_____

Prayer

Dear God, please help me to remember to do the right thing and never act out of stubbornness. I want to be cooperative. Amen.

Paper Hula

Read this to your child: "God doesn't want you to be stubborn. He wants you to be cooperative. Annabel didn't want to wear her winter coat because she really liked her spring jacket a lot. Here is a special skirt that you will like to wear (inside!) whether it's spring or winter. In Hawaii, there is a special dance called the hula. The hula dancers wear skirts made from grass. The skirts sway back and forth when the dancers move. To make your own hula skirt, find a large piece of paper (15" x 25" is a good size). On the 15" side, have your mommy or daddy cut long strips (as shown). Make sure to leave a section of about four inches or so at the top. Fold the top over about an inch, and wrap it around your waist. You can tape it together (or use a paper clip). Now you're ready to do the hula!"

How to cut the strips:

Be Responsible

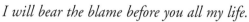

I should accept the blame when I make a mistake.

I will bear the blame before you all my life.
~ Genesis 43:9

Blaming Grandpa

"I'm hungry," said Sierra. "Can I have some cookies?"

Sierra and Grandpa were waiting in the car while Grandma was in the post office. Sierra had spotted a box of cookies in a grocery bag on the front seat.

"I guess so," answered Grandpa as he handed Sierra the box. Sierra happily munched away as they waited for Grandma. She didn't mind that she was dropping a lot of crumbs on the seat. The cookies tasted so good!

When Grandma finally came back to the car, she looked at Sierra and said, "Oh, my, where did you get those cookies?"

"Grandpa," answered Sierra.

"Well, this is a big mess!" said Grandma.

Sierra looked at Grandpa and said, "You're in big trouble now!"

"*You* made the mess with the cookies," said Grandpa.

"But you gave them to me!" said Sierra.

Sierra didn't accept the blame for the mess she had made. She tried to blame Grandpa instead, and that was wrong. God doesn't want you to blame someone else when something is really your fault. He wants you to accept the blame and be responsible for your mistake. Also, be sure to ask the person you hurt, and God, for forgiveness.

Your Turn

1. Why do you think Sierra tried to blame Grandpa for her mess?

_____

_____

2. Tell about a time you blamed someone else when you did wrong.

_____

_____

Prayer

God, please help me to remember that I should take the blame when I do something wrong, and not blame others. I should be responsible. Amen.

Blame Play

Read this to your child: "God wants you to accept the blame when you do something wrong, and never blame others for your mistakes. One way to remember this is to practice what to do in different situations. You can do that by having a puppet play. Here's how. Draw some pictures of people, houses, trees…whatever you like. Cut out the pictures and tape them to craft sticks (pencils or tree sticks work just as well). Sit down beside a table and hold up your puppets so that just the figures show. Now act out different situations where people blame each other or take the blame themselves."

Be Determined

I should do what God says is right, no matter what others tell me.

Do not take advantage of each other.

~ Leviticus 25:17

Wake Up Mommy!

"Go ahead, Vanessa," said Michelle. "Wake up Mommy."

Michelle knew she wasn't supposed to wake up Mommy on Saturday mornings. But this morning Michelle wanted Mommy to read her a book. So she tried to get her little sister, Vanessa, to wake up Mommy for her.

"Go on," said Michelle again to Vanessa. "Wake her up."

"But I don't think I'm supposed to," said Vanessa. "And what if I wake up Daddy then, too? He'll be mad." Vanessa knew the house rules. She didn't want to break them and get in trouble.

Michelle pushed Vanessa toward Mommy's bedroom door as she said, "Wake her up right now!"

Vanessa turned to Michelle and firmly said no, then ran away to her room.

Vanessa did the right thing. She knew Michelle was trying to get her to do something wrong, but no matter how much Michelle tried to get her to do it, Vanessa still said no.

There will always be people who try to get you to do wrong things, but you must still do what is right, as Vanessa did. God teaches in the Bible what is right and wrong. Be determined to do what He says is right, such as following your parents' rules, no matter what other people tell you.

Your Turn

1. Why do you think Michelle didn't want to wake up Mommy herself?

_____

_____

2. Tell about a time someone tried to get you to do something wrong.

_____

_____

Prayer

Dear God, please help me to be determined to do the right thing, and not let other people lead me to do bad things. Amen.

Plants Do the Right Thing

Read this to your child: "There will always be people who try to get you to do wrong things, but just like Vanessa, God wants you to be determined to do what is right. Even plants know that it is good to follow God's rules. To see this, ask Mommy to place a plant in a room that only has one window. Put the plant slightly to one side of the window and water it as you normally would. After a day or two, take a look. Which way is the plant leaning? It will be growing toward the light because it knows that is the best way to grow! No matter how you turn the plant, or where you place it, the plant will always grow toward the light."

Be Unshakable

I should stay away from temptation.

Lead us not into temptation.

~ Matthew 6:13

Take the Cookie

"It's okay," said Ben to his younger sister, Felicity, "take the cookie. No one will ever know."

Felicity looked at the oatmeal cookies on the counter. Mommy had just baked them, and they smelled so good!

"Take one," Ben said again. "Mommy will never know if just one is missing. She didn't count them all."

Felicity knew that Mommy had said not to eat the cookies. She knew that the cookies were for the church bake sale and not for her or her brother.

"Do it," Ben whispered in Felicity's ear. "Just eat one. They're really good."

It was hard for Felicity to say no, but she did. She knew that taking the cookie was wrong, and she didn't want to do something wrong. Even though she was tempted, she did the right thing.

Jesus was tempted, too, when He lived on earth, so He understands how hard it is to do the right thing when you're tempted. But just as He was unshakable when He was tempted, you also can choose to do right when you are tempted.

Your Turn

1. Why did Felicity decide to not eat the cookie?

_____

_____

2. Tell about a time you were tempted to do something that you knew you shouldn't do.

_____

_____

Prayer

God, thank You for understanding how hard it is to be tempted. Please help me to be unshakable and always do the right thing. Amen.

Egg Carton Boat

Read this to your child: "It can be hard to do right when you are tempted to do the wrong thing. God wants you to be unshakable and do the right thing even when you're tempted to do something wrong. Here's an activity that's so much fun, you'll be tempted to play with it all the time! Ask your mommy to save some empty egg cartons. Wash and dry them. Cut the lids off, and hook the cartons together by overlapping the ends or tying them together to make a boat. You can make the boat as long as you like, and decorate it any way you like with crayons, paint or stickers. Float your egg carton boat down a bathtub river, carrying lots of lightweight treasures (paper clips, beads, buttons, etc.). You can experiment with different sizes and weights of cargo for your boat."

Be Kind

I can spread God's love by saying nice things.

Do not keep on babbling.

~ Matthew 6:7

She's Ugly!

Everyone in the car was talking. As the Jones kids and their mom waited in the drive-through line at the restaurant, each kid was pointing out what he or she could see.

Hailey saw a shrub with red berries on it. Sam said he liked the cartoon characters the restaurant had in its windows. Everyone had something to talk about...except Jasmine. She couldn't think of anything to say.

As Mrs. Jones pulled up to the food window, Jasmine felt she should say something. So she said the first thing that came to her mind.

"Look," Jasmine said as she pointed at the clerk, "she's ugly!"

"Jasmine!" Mommy said. "Please tell the lady you're sorry right now."

Jasmine told the clerk she was sorry, but the damage was done. The clerk looked sad because Jasmine said she was ugly. Jasmine had hurt her feelings.

Jasmine didn't mean to hurt the lady at the window. She just wanted to find something to say like the rest of the kids. She didn't think about what she was going to say before she said it, and so she hurt someone's feelings.

God doesn't want you to hurt other people. He wants you to spread His love by saying only nice things. Instead of just babbling on, wait until you have something nice to say. Be kind.

Your Turn

1. Why did Jasmine say that the lady was ugly?

_____

_____

2. Tell about a time you said something wrong to be like everyone else.

_____

_____

Prayer

God, please help me to think before I speak, so that I don't hurt someone's feelings. Help me to be kind. Amen.

Fill-In Puzzle

Read this to your child: "God doesn't want you to hurt other people's feelings, so you should be careful about what you say. He wants you to be kind. Jasmine didn't think about what she was going to say before she said it, and she learned how easily she could hurt someone. What do you think Jasmine ordered at the restaurant? Fill in only the sections below that have the number 3 in them to find out. You can color the picture when you're done."

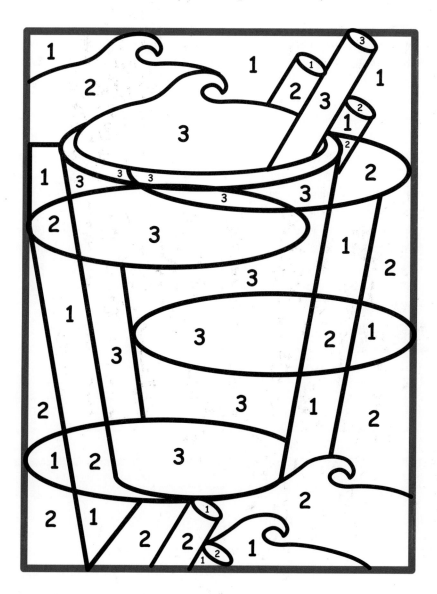

Be Decisive

Sometimes God wants me to decide for myself.

The word of the Lord is flawless.

~ Psalm 18:30

Fuzz Candy

Brooke and her little sister, Bailey, had never seen cotton candy before. When Mommy brought home the big, fluffy cloud of pink candy, they didn't know what to think.

"What's that?" asked Brooke, her eyes wide with excitement.

"It's called cotton candy," answered Mommy. "It tastes sweet. You'll like it."

Brooke touched a tiny bit of the candy to her lip, but before she could taste it, she pulled back. "It's fuzz!" she yelled. "I don't like it!"

Bailey thought the candy felt funny against her lips, too, but she didn't stop there. She put some of the candy into her mouth.

"That's yummy," she said.

Things are not always what they appear. Brooke thought that because the candy was called "cotton" candy and it felt soft and looked fluffy that it must be made of fuzz. You can't always tell what something is by what it's called, or by how it looks or feels.

God wants you to trust Him and your parents to tell you what is right. But sometimes you must also decide for yourself. Don't be tricked into thinking one way or another by what something is called, or how things look. Use what God and your parents have taught you to help you decide for yourself.

Your Turn

1. Why did Brooke think that the cotton candy was made of fuzz?

_____

_____

2. Can you think of some things that aren't how they appear to be?

_____

_____

Prayer

God, please help me to think about things, and not be fooled by how they look or feel. Help me to make the right decisions. Amen.

Paper Pinwheel

Read this to your child: "You should always think things through, and not be fooled by how something looks or feels. Use what God, and your parents, have taught you to help you make good decisions. Some things can become much more than they appear to be, such as this craft. Make four cuts on a square piece of paper from each corner to the center (but not all the way through) as shown in the diagram. Fold the corners toward the center, starting from #1. Secure the center with a pin and push the pin through a straw. Blow on your pinwheel, or face it into the wind to see it spin."

Note to parents: For safety reasons stick a piece of cork onto the sharp end of the pin, but still watch your daughter closely in case she decides to pull it off.

Be Attentive

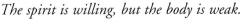

I should do what is right.

The spirit is willing, but the body is weak.

~ Matthew 26:41

Distracting Julia

"Don't clean up," said Cassandra, "this is more fun." Cassandra knew her friend Julia was supposed to be cleaning her room, but she wanted to play with dolls instead.

"I don't know," said Julia. "I don't think I should. Mommy said I should clean my room before I do anything else."

"Okay," said Cassandra, but she made sure that Julia saw her playing with the dolls. No matter how many times Julia tried to clean up, she couldn't help but look back over at Cassandra and her pretty dolls.

When Cassandra dressed one of the dolls in a fancy dress and danced it across the room, Julia stopped cleaning her room and joined in.

Distractions are things that get in the way of doing what you should be doing. Instead of cleaning her room, Julia allowed herself to be distracted into playing with dolls.

There will always be things that take your attention away from being a good Christian. God and your parents teach you what you should and shouldn't do. Pay attention to what you are doing and do the right thing!

Your Turn

1. What was Julia supposed to be doing?

_____

_____

2. How did Cassandra distract Julia?

_____

_____

3. When was a time that you forgot to pay attention?

_____

_____

Prayer

Dear God, help me to pay attention to what I should be doing. Amen.

34

Distracted Water

Read this to your child: "There will always be distractions in your life, but you should never let them take away your attention to what is right. Here is an activity that shows how a spoon distracts water. Go to a sink and turn on the water. Place a spoon into the flow as if you were trying to catch the water in the spoon. You'll notice that the water flows over and around the spoon, but not under it. You can even put your fingers under the spoon and they will stay dry, with just a curtain of water surrounding them."

Be Receptive

People are different & special in their own ways.

Why do you judge your brother?

~ Romans 14:10

Snowflake Similarities

It was the first snow of the winter. Thin blades of green grass poked through the light covering of snow as tiny flakes continued to flutter to the ground.

Katie pressed her face and hands against the living room window. She was filled with joy at seeing the snow. It was so beautiful! How could the world turn white so quickly?

"It's wonderful!" Katie exclaimed.

Katie ran out onto the front porch and scooped up a handful of the cold, white snow. Each flake was different, yet bunched together in her hand, Katie thought they all looked the same. Only after looking very closely at each individual flake could Katie truly see how different they each were.

People, like snowflakes, can look the same, too. It's easy to lump people together into groups, especially when you think they're different from you. However, when you look closely at each person, you'll find that people are different and special in their own ways–just like snowflakes.

God made us each different. Just as no two snowflakes are alike, no two people are alike either. He made us each special, and we are all special to Him. You should be receptive to new friends God sends your way, even if they are different from you.

Your Turn

1. How do snowflakes look when they're all bunched together in your hand?

_____

_____

2. Are any two people the same, or is everyone different?

_____

_____

Prayer

God, help me to be receptive to all of the different and special people you send my way. Amen.

Wax Snowflakes

Read this to your child: "God made people different and special in their own ways. Snowflakes can remind us of people because just as each snowflake is different, so is every person. Have Mommy or Daddy drip melted candle wax into cold water. As it splatters onto the water and cools, it will look like unusual snowflakes."

Be Moderate

I should do everything in moderation.

Eat just enough—too much of it, and you will vomit.

~ Proverbs 25:16

Too Many Stars

"My stomach hurts," said Daddy, as he rubbed his tummy with his hand. "Why does your stomach hurt?" asked Mommy.

"I ate a whole bag of chocolate stars for lunch," said Daddy, grinning.

After Daddy left, Maria asked Mommy, "Why does Daddy get to eat chocolate for lunch, and I never can?"

"I don't want you to feel sick like Daddy, that's why," answered Mommy. "Daddy ate way too many chocolate stars and now he's feeling sick because of it. He did something that was bad for his body, and now he's paying for it by feeling sick."

Maria's daddy made himself sick by eating too many chocolate stars. He shouldn't have eaten candy for his lunch, and he shouldn't have eaten so many. It wasn't good for his body.

Too much of a good thing can be bad. God gives us many good things, but if we use them wrong, or take too much of them, good things can actually become bad. God wants you to use the brain He has given you to decide how, why and when to use the things in this world, so that you don't hurt others or yourself.

Your Turn

1. Why was candy a bad lunch for Daddy?

_____

_____

2. Tell about a time you ate too much of something and then felt badly because of it.

_____

_____

Prayer

Dear God, please help me to remember that I shouldn't take too much of anything. I should do everything in moderation. Amen.

Homemade Frozen Pops

Read this to your child: "God wants you to use what He gives you in a correct way. You should never take too much of anything, because that could be bad for you. Here's something that tastes good, but don't take too many or you might get a tummy-ache like Maria's daddy! Ask Mommy or Daddy for an empty ice cube tray. Pour in juice instead of water, insert a toothpick into each square, and freeze. After the pops are frozen, pull a cube out by gripping a toothpick. You have made your own frozen pops!"

Be Organized

If I am organized I can serve God better.

There is a proper time and procedure for every matter.

~ Ecclesiastes 8:6

Hurry Up

"Hurry up and finish," called Mommy. "We don't have much time left."

Frances was coloring a picture for her Sunday school teacher. She was hurrying to get it done before she had to leave.

"I'm almost done," Frances called back. "I just have to fill in a couple of parts."

"Frances," Mommy said, "you know you should have done this last night. Or you could have gotten up earlier this morning to finish it. I'm afraid you'll just have to leave it until next Sunday now."

"No," cried Frances. "I want to give it to her today!"

"I'm sorry, Frances," answered Mommy, "there just isn't time."

You cannot make time for everything. That's why it is good to organize your time carefully. Frances didn't organize her time well. She could have worked on her picture the night before or gotten up early, but she didn't.

Frances didn't organize her time, so she couldn't finish her picture. In the same way, you have to organize your time to serve God. Be sure to organize you time well so you can pray, go to church, read Bible stories and tell others about God. If you are careful, you will have plenty of time in your life to do all of the things that are important to you.

Your Turn

1. Why didn't Frances get the picture done?

_____

_____

2. How do you organize your time to serve God better?

_____

_____

Prayer

Thank You, God, for giving me so much time. Please help me to always organize it well. Amen.

Organizing a Picture Garden

Read this to your child: "God gives you a certain amount of time, so you need to organize it well. Frances didn't get her picture done because she didn't organize her time. If you organize all of the items you need for this activity, and wait until you have some free time, you can finish this picture with no trouble at all!"

What You Need

construction paper
glue
crayons
cupcake baking cups
chenille wire
glitter

What to Do

1. Place the construction paper on a flat surface.
2. Show your daughter how to form flowers on the construction paper using the cupcake papers as flowers and chenille wire as stems. Also, you can cut the baking cups into sections to make leaves.
3. Allow your daughter to "organize" her picture garden, then help her glue the items into place on the construction paper.
4. Encourage your daughter to finish her picture garden using crayons and/or glitter.

Be Healthy

I must wisely use everything God gives me.

They were responsible for…their use.

~ Numbers 3:31

More Vitamins!

"I want more vitamins!" Crystal cried. She loved the way her vitamins tasted. They were sweet like candy. She only wished she could have more than one a day.

"No more," said Mommy.

"But vitamins are good for me," Crystal said. "I should have more so I can be extra healthy."

"That's not how it works," explained Mommy. "Vitamins are only good for you if you take them like you're supposed to take them. You should never eat more than I give you."

"Why not?" asked Crystal.

"Because if you ate more than I gave you," said Mommy, "I would have to take you to the hospital right away. You would get very sick. You wouldn't feel good. You would feel bad."

God gives you many wonderful things to help you, but if you don't use them wisely, they can hurt you, too. Medicine is good for you when you go by the directions. But medicine can be harmful if you use it incorrectly. Let Mommy or Daddy help you with medicine. And be thankful to God for creating things to help you be healthy.

Your Turn

1. What kind of medicine do you take?

_____

_____

2. Who created medicine?

_____

_____

Prayer

Thank You, God, for giving me medicine to make me feel better. Amen.

Vinegar Bone

Read this to your child: "As Crystal learned, sometimes good things can be bad when they are used unwisely. Vinegar is a good example of that. Vinegar can be used in cooking, but if you use too much vinegar for too long, it can be harmful. To see how this works, place a chicken bone in a jar of vinegar. Replace the vinegar every few days. After a couple of weeks, the hard bone will begin to get soft because that much vinegar is not good for the bone."

Be Yourself

I should be myself.

Keep yourself pure.

~ 1 Timothy 5:22

Covers

"So that's what the bed really looks like," Shelby said as she watched Mommy take the covers off her big sister Angie's bed. It sure looked different with the blankets and sheets gone. The mattress had pretty blue and white stripes on it, and it felt like satin.

"It's prettier this way," said Shelby. "We should leave it like that."

As Shelby and Mommy bundled up the sheets and blankets to carry to the washing machine, Angie walked into the room. "My bed!" she cried. "What happened? My bed has no skin on it!"

Shelby laughed. "I like it better this way," she said.

"Well, I don't," said Angie. "Let's put my sheets back on!"

Sometimes people pretend that they are something they're not. Like the bed with the sheets and blankets on it, they look different than they really are underneath. But God made you beautiful and wonderful inside, so you don't need to hide under covers. He loves you just the way you are.

Shelby knew that Angie's bed was prettier underneath all the sheets and blankets. You are, too!

Your Turn

1. Why did Shelby think the bed was prettier without sheets and blankets on it?

_____

_____

2. Do you ever pretend to be different than you really are? Why or why not?

_____

_____

Prayer

Dear God, please help me to remember that I'm wonderful just as I am. Amen.

Under the Covers

Read this to your child: "God doesn't want you to act like you're something you're not. He loves you just as you are. You don't need to cover up who you really are inside. Here are some things that we sometimes cover up. Can you match the cover to the thing it covers? Draw a line to connect them."

I Can Live God's Way

Mistakes

God understands that I sometimes make mistakes.

We all stumble in many ways.

~ James 3:2

Mistaken Identity

Brittany had a problem. Every time she filled her bird feeder, she woke up the next day to find it empty again. Sometimes the feeder would be all covered with mud, too. Where were the sunflower seeds going?

"A cocoon ate the seeds," said Brittany's little sister, Kaitlyn.

"That doesn't make sense," said Brittany. "A cocoon is what a caterpillar makes before it turns into a butterfly. It doesn't eat seeds out of bird feeders."

"Yes it does," Kaitlyn said again. "Mommy and Daddy told me so."

Brittany tried to imagine a giant caterpillar weaving its cocoon around her bird feeder at night, and then eating all of the seeds before morning. Could that really be what was happening?

Later that day, Brittany heard Mommy say, "I hope that raccoon doesn't come back again tonight. Every time he eats the birdseed, he gets his muddy feet all over everything. He's a very messy eater."

Oh, thought Brittany, *now it all makes sense*. It wasn't a "cocoon" but a "raccoon" that was eating all the seed. Kaitlyn had just made a mistake.

Kaitlyn didn't lie to Brittany when she said a cocoon had eaten the sunflower seeds. She had simply misunderstood when Mommy said "raccoon." God understands when you make mistakes. He wants you to do your best to tell the truth, but He knows that sometimes mistakes happen.

Your Turn

1. What did Kaitlyn think was eating the seed?

_____

_____

2. Tell about a time when you made a mistake.

_____

_____

Prayer

Thank You, God, for understanding when I make mistakes. Amen.

Fill the Feeder

Read this to your child: "Brittany's mistake was an easy one to make. It might be easy to make mistakes in the maze below, too. Be careful as you help Brittany find her way to her bird feeder so she can fill it with seed."

Willingness

I should do things willingly.

Whoever turns a sinner from the error of his way will save him.
~ James 5:20

Haircut Day

Chelsea hated having her hair cut, so when Mommy told Chelsea it was time to trim her hair, Chelsea wasn't happy.

"I haven't been getting many points lately when I play soccer," said Chelsea, "and I think it's because the sun gets in my eyes. If you let my hair get long then the hair will keep the sun from shining in my eyes."

Mommy laughed at Chelsea's serious face. "I think it's more likely that having a haircut will help your game," said Mommy. "A haircut will keep that long hair from getting in your eyes, so you'll be able to see the ball better."

"But having my hair in my eyes is good," answered Chelsea. "That's what keeps the sun out."

Sometimes when people don't want to do something, they make up reasons for why they shouldn't do it. Chelsea was trying very hard to find reasons to keep Mommy from cutting her hair, even though those reasons were silly.

God doesn't want you to make up reasons not to do what you should do. If you are afraid to do something, then you should trust God (and your parents) to know what's best.

Your Turn

1. Do you like having your hair cut? Why or why not?

_____

_____

2. How can you know if you are doing something for the right reasons?

_____

_____

Prayer

Dear God, please help me to remember that making up silly reasons to avoid doing what I should do doesn't make You happy. I trust You, God. Amen.

What You Don't Like

Read this to your child: "God wants you to do what you should without making up silly excuses. Here are some things that people sometimes avoid doing. Draw a circle around the ones that you don't like to do. Talk with Mommy or Daddy about why you don't like to do the things you circled."

Focus

I should take my time to do my best.

Do not abandon the works of your hands.

~ Psalm 138:8

Cheese and Crackers

Janeesa carefully looked at the cheese and crackers in front of her. She was very hungry, and could almost taste the salty, crisp cracker and feel the smooth, creamy cheese on her tongue. Janeesa worked slowly to spread the cheese across her cracker, careful to go right up to the edge of the cracker, but not past it.

When Mommy noticed that it was taking Janeesa a long time to get her cracker ready to eat, she asked, "Why don't you just slap some cheese into the middle of the cracker and eat it?"

"No, no," said Janeesa, never looking up from what she was doing. "That would make a mess."

"But it would be faster," said Mommy.

"No," said Janeesa again. "That wouldn't be the right way. I don't like it that way." She continued to smooth the cheese over every part of her cracker. Only when the cracker was completely and evenly covered did Janeesa finally lift the cracker to her mouth to eat it.

Even though she was very hungry, Janeesa took the time to do a good job of covering her cracker with the cheese before she ate it. Because Janeesa waited, the cracker tasted extra good. Doing a good job was worth the wait! God also wants you to do a good job at whatever you're doing. Taking the time to do a good job is well worth it. God will be proud of you for doing your best.

Your Turn

1. Why was it taking Janeesa a long time to put cheese on her cracker?

_____

_____

2. When you're doing something, do you do it the "right" or the fastest way?

_____

_____

Prayer

God, please help me to remember that doing something right is worth the wait. Amen.

Egg Basket

Read this to your child: "Doing things the right way is the way God wants you to do things. Take your time to do this project, and you'll be happy to see how nice it looks when you're done. Cut the lid off of an empty egg carton, and cut the carton in half. Have your Mommy or Daddy make a short, straight cut in each side of the carton (as shown). Now take a strip of cardboard, thread each end through the cuts in each side of the egg carton, and fold up on the inside so that the cardboard doesn't slip out of place. Now you have a pretty little basket in which to store lightweight things."

Make a straight cut on both sides of the carton.

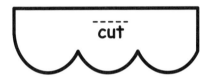

cut

Fold a strip of cardboard and slide it into each slit.

fold   fold

Enjoy your new Egg Basket!

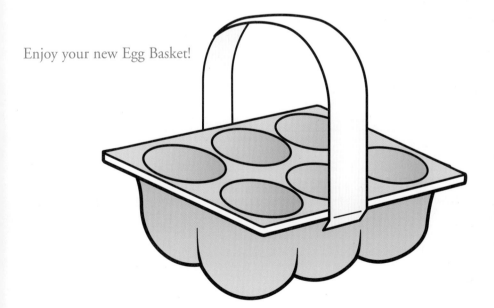

Pretending

I have to act to make something happen.

With God all things are possible.

~ Matthew 19:26

I'm Calmed Down!

Ashley had done a naughty thing. She had pushed her little sister and made her fall down. Mommy sent Ashley to the time-out corner. Ashley was mad. She screamed and cried and banged her feet on the floor. When a few minutes passed and Mommy still didn't let Ashley come out of the corner, Ashley started to pound her fists on the floor and yell.

Mommy told Ashley that she couldn't come out of the time-out corner until she had been quiet for a whole minute, but Ashley just kept yelling. "If you don't calm down," said Mommy, "I'm not going to let you out of the corner."

Ashley thought about what Mommy said. She took a deep breath, kicked her feet and screamed as loud as she could, "I'm calmed down! I'm calmed down! I'm calmed down!"

Ashley thought that she didn't have to really be "calmed down" as long as she said she was, but just saying something doesn't make it so. If you want something to be real, you have to really do it. Just pretending or wishing for something to happen won't make it real.

God tells us that with Him all things are possible. If you want to do something, you can do it if you really try. Even if something is hard to do, with God helping you, you can make it happen. Ashley was having a hard time calming down, but if she had prayed to God, it would have been easier.

Your Turn

1. What did Mommy tell Ashley to do if she wanted to get out of the corner?

_____

_____

2. Does saying something is so make it real?

_____

_____

Prayer

God, with You all things are possible. When I want something to happen, please help me to do the right thing to make it happen. Amen.

Praying for Calm

Read this to your child: "Maybe if Ashley had prayed to God, calming down would have been easier. Here's a picture for you to color of Ashley praying while she sits in the corner."

Striving

God wants me to work hard.

The work of his hands rewards him.

~ Proverbs 12:14

Hard Work

Alexa quietly watched as Mommy dug in the flower bed. She loved to see Mommy pull out the weeds and cut off the dead flowers.

As Mommy loosened the dirt with her small rake, Alexa suddenly noticed something that she hadn't seen before. Lots and lots of ants had suddenly appeared and were running everywhere. *Where had they all come from?* she wondered. Just a moment before there hadn't been any there.

Mommy explained to Alexa that ants live underground in long tunnels that they dig out of the dirt. "I must have hit one of their tunnels with my rake," she said, "so now the ants are hurrying to fix the mess that my rake made."

"But why?" asked Alexa. "Why are they all trying to fix the tunnels when they could be running away? Aren't they scared?"

"Ants don't let anything or anyone stop them from doing their work," said Mommy. "Ants are a good example of hard work. They strive hard."

Ants never run away or play when there's work to be done. God wants you to be that way, too. He wants you to strive to help when you can, especially when you do His work and tell a friend about Him.

Your Turn

1. Why did the ants start running around suddenly?

_____

_____

2. Do you strive to work as hard as ants do? Why or why not?

_____

_____

Prayer

Dear God, please help me to remember that I should strive to do my best and work hard. Amen.

Counting Ants

Read this to your child: "Ants are a good example of hard work. God wants us to strive to work hard, too. Here are some ants who are working hard to build their ant hills. Can you count how many ants are on each hill? Connect the anthill to the correct number."

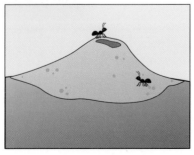

Thrifty

I should use wisely all that God gives me.

Each one should use whatever gift he has received to serve others.

~ 1 Peter 4:10

The Land of Many Eggs

"Eggs again!" moaned Blair. "Why do I have to eat eggs again?"

"Because now," answered Mommy with a smile, "we live in the land of many eggs."

Blair giggled. Mommy was talking about how their chickens had just begun laying eggs every day.

When Daddy first brought home the box full of fuzzy baby chicks, it was hard to believe that someday they'd be big enough to lay eggs. Blair and her sisters loved to pet the chicks' soft, yellow feathers, and snuggle them close.

But now the tiny chicks had grown into big chickens, clucking and scratching around in the yard. Twice a day, Blair and her sisters hunted for eggs, and already they had been finding two each day. Daddy said that soon they'd find 24 eggs every day! What would they do with all those eggs?

"We can't waste them," said Mommy. "We should never waste food."

Blair's mommy was right. God gives you many things, and you should never be wasteful. You should use everything that God gives you in the best possible way. If you have too much, you should share with someone who needs it.

Your Turn

1. Why should Blair not waste the eggs?

_____

_____

2. Have you ever wasted anything? Why or why not?

_____

_____

Prayer

God, thank You for everything You've given me. Please help me to remember that I should never waste anything. Amen.

Egg Uses

Read this to your child: "God doesn't want you to waste anything that He's given you, even if you have too much of something. Blair has too many eggs. What are some ways that she could use all those eggs? Circle the ways the eggs can be used."

Learning

God wants me to always be learning.

Choose…knowledge rather than choice gold.

~ Proverbs 8:10

Every Time Is Learning Time

Kimberly pushed the toy baby buggy back and forth in Grandma's basement, careful to be gentle with the three baby dolls inside.

When Grandma saw what Kimberly was doing, she knew that it was a good opportunity to teach Kimberly something new. "How many dolls are in your buggy?" asked Grandma as she knelt down beside Kimberly.

Kimberly looked down into the buggy, and slowly started to count. "One, two, three. Three!" answered Kimberly.

"That's very good," said Grandma as she put another baby doll inside the basket. "Now how many babies do you see?" asked Grandma.

"One, two, three," began Kimberly, "and four!"

"Very good," said Grandma. "I'm so proud of you, Kimberly. You counted those baby dolls just right."

Any time can be a good time to learn something new or to practice something you already know. Kimberly and Grandma were having fun playing, but they found that they could also practice numbers at the same time.

God wants you to learn as much as you can so that you are the best that you can be, even when you're just playing. Every time can be learning time!

Your Turn

1. How did Grandma help Kimberly to learn something?

_____

_____

2. When you are playing, do you ever learn something new, too?

_____

_____

Prayer

Dear God, please help me to learn new things all the time, even when I'm just playing. Amen.

Counting Babies

Read this to your child: "God wants you to always be learning, even when you are just playing. Kimberly counted her baby dolls very well. Can you do the same? Draw a line from the dolls to the correct number."

Trying

I should try as hard as I can.

Your work will be rewarded.

~ 2 Chronicles 15:7

There's Too Much!

"There's too much," said Autumn. "I can't ever learn it all."

"What do you mean?" Mommy asked.

Autumn sighed. "I mean it seems like you're always telling me something new. There are just too many things to learn. I'll never learn it all!"

"Well of course you'll never learn it all," said Mommy. "You're not supposed to know everything–only God knows everything. But you should do your best to learn as much as you can about the world."

"But there's so much," Autumn said again. "Yesterday, Daddy told me that moths are different from butterflies…and Davey said that there are more different countries in the world than I can count on my fingers…and you told me today that grapes don't grow on trees. There's just too much!"

Mommy laughed. "I know it seems like a lot," said Mommy, "but if you try a little bit more every day, even when you don't realize that you're learning, you sometimes are. All that's important is that you try your best. That's what God asks of you."

God gave you a brain to make you smart. You can learn a lot, and you should try your best every day. Only by trying as hard as you can will you be the best person that you can be–the kind of person God wants you to be.

Your Turn

1. What kinds of things did Autumn say she had just learned?

_____

_____

2. Do you try hard to learn each day? What did you try hard to do today?

_____

_____

Prayer

God, please help me to always try as hard as I can. Amen.

Yeast Lesson

Read this to your child: "God made everything in the world. The world is so full of amazing things that you could never learn everything about it. You need to always try your best if you're to learn as much as you can. Here's an activity that will teach you a surprising thing about yeast. Yeast looks like little pieces of dirt or grain, but it's really alive! Mix a cup of water, a tablespoon of sugar, and one cup of flour together. Divide the mixture into two bowls. In one bowl only, add one teaspoon of yeast. Let the bowls sit in a warm place for about an hour. Look at the bowls. Only the bowl with the yeast will be bubbly—that's because the yeast is actually eating the sugar and giving off a chemical called carbon dioxide. Now you've learned about yeast!"

Patience

God wants me to be patient while I learn.

If we hope for what we do not yet have, we wait for it patiently.

~ Romans 8:25

Trying Again

"Ohh," yelled Lola. "I can't do it. I can't do it!"

"What's the matter?" Lola's mommy asked as she walked into the room.

"I can't get these on," Lola cried. Lola had just gotten some new slippers from Grandma, but she couldn't get them on. Every time she managed to get one on, her heel would slip back out.

Lola's mommy bent down to look at the slippers. "Well here's the problem," she said. "You've got two pairs of socks on. You need to take off the socks and then try again."

"But I don't want to try again!" Lola whined, as she threw the slippers.

Mommy sat beside Lola and took her hand. "Remember when you couldn't get your seat belt on in the car?" she asked. "You tried and tried, and you were crying because you didn't think you could do it. Remember all you had to do was calm down, and start over."

Lola thought about what Mommy said, took a deep breath, pulled off her socks and tried to put the slippers on again.

"I did it!" she called with a smile. "I really did it!"

Sometimes it's hard to keep trying. If something doesn't work the first time, it can seem easier to just give up. God teaches us that patience is a good thing. He wants you to give yourself time to learn new things, and not get upset just because it doesn't work the first time. Be patient!

Your Turn

1. Why was Lola upset?

_____

_____

2. Can you think of a time when you needed to be patient?

_____

_____

Prayer

God, please help me to be patient. Amen.

Find Lola's Slippers

Read this to your child: "God teaches that patience is a good thing. Can you be patient long enough to find your way through this maze?"

Curiosity

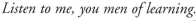

I should use my curiosity for good.

Listen to me, you men of learning.

~ Job 34:2

Curious Amber

Amber slowly walked down the aisle at the pet shop. Her big brother, Peter, watched as she looked at all the shiny bird cages, pretty cat toys and tiny fish in the big aquariums.

Amber didn't touch anything until she came to the dog food. There were four clear containers of dog food pellets, each in a different color. Peter could see that Amber wanted to reach out and grab a handful of the pretty pellets.

"No, no," said Peter as he pointed to the dog food. "Don't touch."

Amber knew she shouldn't touch the dog food. Peter had told her not to, but she really wanted to anyway. So when Peter turned to look at some fish, Amber grabbed a piece of the green dog food and put it in her mouth.

When Peter saw the green, gooey mess around Amber's mouth, he ran to tell his Mommy. "What should we do?" he asked.

Mommy told the store clerk what had happened, and they cleaned out Amber's mouth as best they could.

It's good to be curious. God gave you curiosity to make you want to learn new things. But curiosity can be bad when you let it lead you to do bad things. Amber let her curiosity lead her to eat dog food, which could have made her sick. Use your curiosity to learn good things!

Your Turn

1. What did Amber put in her mouth?

_____

_____

2. What has made you curious? Did it end up good or bad?

_____

_____

Prayer

Dear God, thank You for giving me curiosity. Please help me to always be curious in a good way. Amen.

Good and Bad Curiosity

Read this to your child: "God wants us to be curious, but in good ways. We should never let curiosity lead us to do something bad. Here are some things that make people curious. Mark an 'X' over the ones that you think could lead to doing something bad. Circle the good ones."

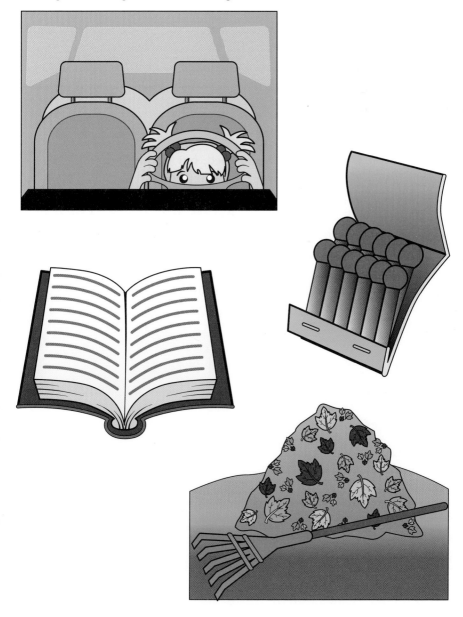

Responsibility
I should be responsible.

You are responsible for the wrong I am suffering.
~ Genesis 16:5

Erika's Bedtime

Erika knew that she was supposed to go to bed at 7:00. She knew that it was important for her body to get enough sleep so that it could grow big and strong. It was Erika's job to make sure she went to bed when she was supposed to, but she didn't want to go to bed. She wanted to play.

"Where's Erika?" Mommy asked Daddy as she looked around the house. "I can't find her."

Mommy and Daddy searched all over the house looking for Erika. Finally, Daddy found her outside on the front porch.

"I don't want to go to bed," Erika cried, but Daddy carried her into her bedroom anyway. He scolded her for hiding outside, and reminded her of how important it was for her to get her sleep.

We all have responsibilities–things we need to make sure we do. Even if you don't like what you're supposed to do, you still need to do it. Erika thought that she could run away and hide from her responsibility, but she couldn't. God is always watching to make sure you keep your responsibilities. Just like Erika couldn't run away from Daddy, you cannot run away from God.

Your Turn

1. Was Erika able to run away from her responsibility?

_____

_____

2. Do you have responsibilities? What are they?

_____

_____

Prayer

God, thank You for giving me responsibilities. Please help me to do the right thing, and to never run away from my responsibilities. Amen.

Flying Streamers

Read this to your child: "God wants you to never run away from your responsibilities as Erika did, but here's something that's fun to run away from. Find a stick or an unsharpened pencil and tie a long piece of crepe paper on the end. Wave the pencil through the air or 'write' numbers in the air. Whatever you do with the stick or pencil, the streamer will follow. It's fun! You can experiment with different lengths of crepe paper."

Priorities

I always should do first what is important.

The important thing is that…Christ is preached.

~ Philemon 1:18

First Things First

Emily had silky black hair and the most beautiful blue eyes anyone had ever seen. When she smiled, her eyes showed joy, and her giggle was pure magic. She was simply one of the best friends Lynne had ever had.

The first time Lynne met Emily was when Lynne's family went to dinner at Emily's house. Lynne's mommy helped Lynne make one of her favorite desserts–chocolate pudding with candy worms "crawling" across the top of the dish. Yum, yum!

When Emily saw the dessert, she didn't care about the pudding–she just wanted some of those worms! They were green and red and yucky-looking, but they tasted very, very good.

Emily ate one worm, but when she reached for another, her mommy said, "No, Emily, eat your dinner first." Emily just wanted to eat worms!

Emily picked at her chicken and rice at first, but then she finally ate it. When dinner was done, Lynne and Emily got to eat all the worms their tummies could hold.

It's always best to do the most important things first. Emily's mommy knew it was important for Emily to eat the food her body needed first. God wants you to have good priorities and do what's most important first. The most important thing you can do is tell others about Him.

Your Turn

1. Do you always eat the food your body needs before you eat treats? Why?

_____

_____

2. Why does God want you to do the important things first?

_____

_____

Prayer

Thank You, God, for helping me to know what is most important to do first. Amen.

Dirty Worms

Read this to your child: "It's best that you do the most important things first, like eat good food, and then with the time that's left over you can play or have treats. Here's how to make the treat that Lynne and Emily liked so much:"

What You Need

❈ 1 package chocolate instant pudding
❈ 1 8-oz. container whipped topping
❈ 1½ cups milk
❈ 30 chocolate sandwich cookies, crushed
❈ candy worms or candy bugs.

What to Do

1. Mix the pudding mix and milk together. Let it stand for a couple minutes.
2. Slowly fold in the whipped topping.
3. Spread a layer of cookies in the bottom of a container (use short glasses to make individual servings)
4. Add a layer of the pudding mixture.
5. Top with more cookies (make as many layers as you want).
6. Place candy worms or bugs on the top so it looks like they're crawling out of the "dirt."

Acceptance

God wants me to make the best of everything.

I am the Lord your God, who teaches you what is best for you.

~ Isaiah 48:17

I'm the Baby!

Mommy was in the hospital. Alexandra was staying with Grandma while Mommy was away. Alexandra knew that when she returned home there would be a new baby there.

"Pretty soon you'll have a new baby sister or brother," said Grandma.

"No!" cried Alexandra, "I'm the baby!" Alexandra felt sad that she would no longer be the baby in the family.

"But you'll love the new baby," answered Grandma. "You'll see."

Alexandra didn't believe Grandma…until she saw her baby sister. Victoria was small, cuddly and so cute! When Alexandra touched the baby's hand, Victoria tightly gripped it. Alexandra liked that! Looking at the new baby, Alexandra couldn't understand why she was ever sad about it.

If Alexandra had kept on being sad about having a new baby sister, just think how much she would have missed. She never would have seen how cute her sister was, or felt her sister's tiny hand holding hers. Accepting that she wasn't the baby in the family anymore turned out to be a good thing!

God doesn't want you to waste your time being sad about things you can't change. He wants you to spend your time making the things you can change better. If you make the best of the things that you can't change, and work on the things that you can, the world will be a better place for everyone.

Your Turn

1. Why didn't Alexandra want a new baby?

_____

_____

2. How did you (or how would you) feel about a new baby in your family?

_____

_____

Prayer

God, please help me to make the best of the things that I can't change. Amen.

Can...or Can't?

Read this to your child: "God doesn't want you to waste your time being sad about things that you can't change. Here are some things that you can't change, and some that you can. Do you know which are which? Cross out the ones that you can't change, and circle the ones that you can."

Economy

I should use faithfully all that God gives me.

Let us be thankful.

~ Hebrews 12:38

Lacey the Vacuum Cleaner

"Where's my pretzel?" asked Josh. He had left his pretzel on the table while he went to look at something on TV. "It was here a minute ago."

"I don't know," Mommy said. "Maybe Lacey ate it."

Josh got another pretzel, but when he sat it down to go answer the phone, it disappeared.

"Now where did my pretzel go?" Josh hollered.

Daddy heard Josh from the living room and called, "Maybe Lacey ate it."

Later that day, when Josh left the table to get a napkin, he came back to find his carrots gone. "Hey," Josh cried, "where did my carrots go?"

Josh looked over to see his little sister, Lacey, sitting on the floor, munching away on something orange. "Did you eat my carrots?" Josh asked.

Lacey just looked at Josh and kept chewing.

Lacey became known as the "vacuum cleaner" in her family because whatever food was left on the table, she would quickly swoop up and eat. No food was ever wasted in their family as long as Lacey was around.

Mommy liked that Lacey helped the family not to be wasteful. God doesn't want you to waste what He gives you, including food.

Your Turn

1. Why did Mommy like that Lacey ate the leftovers?

_____

_____

2. Can you think of some ways that you can use all that God gives you?

_____

_____

Prayer

Thank You, God, for giving me so many wonderful things, including food to eat. Please help me to remember that I should always use all that You give me. Amen.

What Did She Eat?

Read this to your child: "God doesn't want you to waste anything. He wants you to make good use of all that He gives you. Lacey helped her family not to waste any food. Color the sections of the picture below that have the number 2 in them to see something that Lacey ate. You can color the picture when you're done."

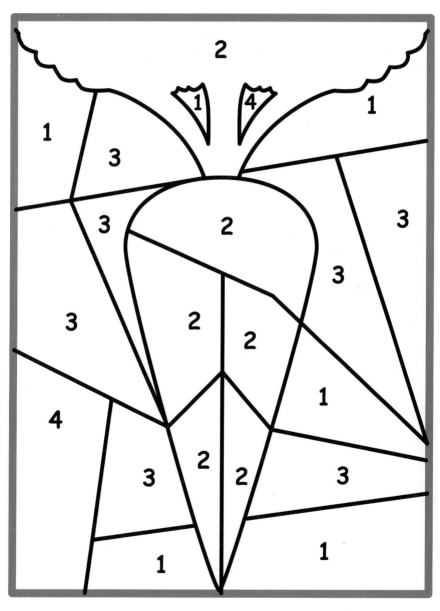

Judgment

I should not judge others.

A prudent man gives thought to his steps.

~ Proverbs 14:15

That Guy's Crazy!

Ella sat in front of the television, watching the evening news. There was a long story about a man who didn't leave when a big storm was coming, and his house was torn to pieces. The TV reporter talked to the man as he stood outside what was left of his house. Not only was his home gone, his daughter was missing. She had been lost in the storm.

"That guy's crazy!" said Ella.

"Now Ella," said Mommy, "you don't know that. Maybe he had a good reason for staying at his house during the storm, or maybe he couldn't leave for some reason."

Ella thought about it, but said again, "That guy's crazy."

As the report went on, Ella soon learned that the man had stayed because his daughter had been lost before the storm hit. He needed to stay in case she came back so he could help her.

Sometimes it seems easy to judge other people, but God doesn't want you to judge. Only He knows why people make the choices they do, and only He should judge people.

Your Turn

1. Why did the man stay in his house even though the bad storm was coming?

_____

_____

2. Why should you never judge other people?

_____

_____

Prayer

Dear God, please help me to remember that I should never judge other people. Only You know why people do what they do, and only You should judge. Amen.

Bottle Storm

Read this to your child: "Only God should judge people, because only He knows why people really do what they choose to do. The man on TV had been through a very bad storm. Here's a way to make your own storm. Find two empty two-liter bottles. Fill one with water and tape the two together at the openings (make sure the seal is very tight). Now flip the bottle over and twist back and forth. It will look like a storm!"

Interpretation

God wants me to think the best of people & the world.

Everyone has…an interpretation.

~ 1 Corinthians 14:26

The Chicken Kiss

Cousin Steven was visiting Tara and Kristin while his mommy was at work, so he had to help with the daily chores. One of the jobs they needed to do was take care of the chickens. Tara carried the bucket out for Steven as he and Aunt Laura gathered the eggs, then Steven decided that he'd like to feed the chickens some corn.

Steven held the cob of corn through the fence as the chickens pecked at it. He loved how they pecked so hard that he almost lost his hold on the cob. He was having fun when suddenly one of the chickens pecked his finger.

Steven looked like he was going to cry, but Aunt Laura quickly said, "Wow, Steven, did you get a chicken kiss?"

When Steven heard that, he began to smile again, and continued to have fun feeding the chickens.

Steven was going to cry when he thought the chicken had bitten him. But when he thought that the chicken had kissed him, he smiled. How he felt about what the chicken did depended upon how he interpreted it. A bite hurts, but a kiss is wonderful!

God gives you a wonderful world to live in. Bad things sometimes happen, but a lot depends on what you think about them. Just like Steven, if you see things in a good way, you'll be happier. God wants you to think the best about the world, and the people who live in it.

Your Turn

1. Why did Steven look like he was going to cry?

_____

_____

2. Do you think you would have cried or smiled if a chicken pecked you?

_____

_____

Prayer

Dear God, please help me to look at Your world in a good way. Amen.

Good and Bad

Read this to your child: "God wants you to look at the world, and the people in it, in the best possible way. Bad things can happen, but sometimes what seems bad can be good depending on how you look at it. Look at the pictures below. Each can be bad or good. Talk with your mommy or daddy about the ways in which each is both bad and good depending on how you look at it. Finish coloring the pictures when you're done."

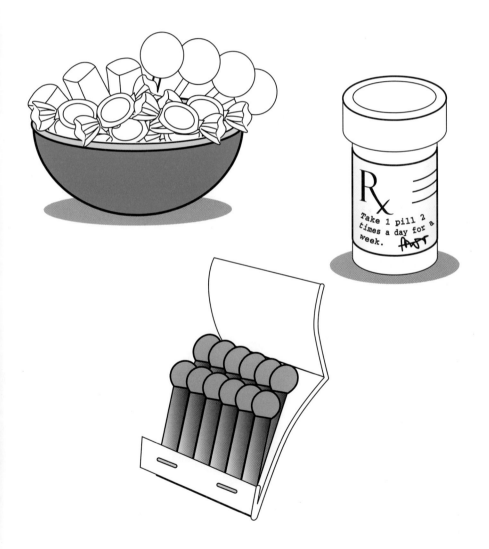

Imagination

God gives me imagination.

Think about it! Consider it! Tell us what to do!

~ Judges 19:30

Abby's World

"Cars can go 300 miles an hour in my world," said Abby with a smile.

"In your world?" asked Mommy.

"Yes," said Abby. "In my pretend world we've taken the wheels and gas out of cars and now they run on electricity and float on air. The air props it up so that the car floats." Abby was proud of her ideas.

"It sounds like you've got it all figured out," said Mommy.

"Yeah," answered Abby, "that's my world in the year 4001."

"Well, I'm sure you'll make the world an even better place to live in with all your ideas when you grow up," said Mommy as she gave Abby a big hug.

Abby had a good imagination, and that's a wonderful thing. God gives you an imagination so you can be creative and happy. Without imagination, inventors would never have thought of things like telephones, computers and cars. Imagination is one of the best gifts God gives you!

Your Turn

1. What made Abby able to think of all her ideas?

_____

_____

2. Have you imagined any new things?

_____

_____

3. Who gives you imagination?

_____

Prayer

Thank You, God, for Your gift of imagination. Amen.

Abby's Car

Read this to your child: "God gives you an imagination so you can be happier, healthier and think of new things to make the world a better place. Here's a picture of the car that Abby imagined. Finish coloring it, then draw yourself inside it!"

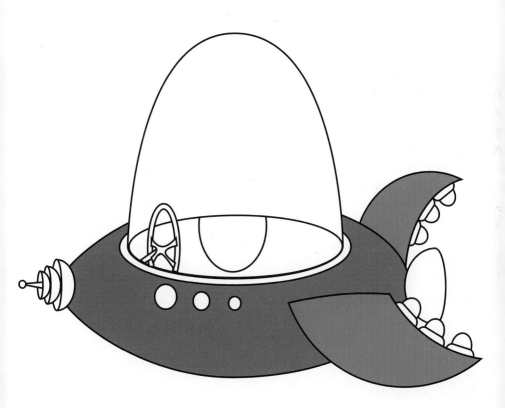

Control

Having control helps me follow God's rules.

If the Lord is God, follow him.

~ 1 Kings 18:21

Baby Deer

Daddy motioned with his hand for Natalie to come over. He was standing by the edge of the forest near their house, pointing down at something. As Natalie drew closer, Daddy put his finger to his lips as a way to tell Natalie to be very quiet.

When Natalie saw what Daddy was looking at, she couldn't believe her eyes! There, lying in the grass at Daddy's feet, was a baby deer. The spotted fawn just looked at Natalie and Daddy as they bent down to pet her. The fawn lay very still as Natalie stroked her soft, brown fur. Natalie could feel the happiness getting bigger and bigger inside her, and even though she knew she needed to be quiet, she just couldn't help it–a squeal of joy came squeaking out.

"Baa," blurted the fawn as it jumped up and ran toward the woods. Natalie was very sad that she had scared away the fawn, but she just couldn't control herself. She had been so excited that she couldn't keep from making a sound, and her squeal was scary for the tiny fawn, so she ran away.

Natalie scared away the fawn because she couldn't control her feelings. But as you grow up, you'll learn to control yourself better. For example, you'll control your voice in church so that you're quiet, and you'll control emotions, too, so that you don't yell at people when you're angry. Having control will help you follow the rules God has given you. Ask God to help you learn to have more control.

Your Turn

1. Why did Daddy want Natalie to be quiet by the fawn?

_____

_____

2. In what ways do you control yourself?

_____

_____

Prayer

God, please help me to control myself. Amen.

Cut-Out Picture

Read this to your child: "As you grow up, you should learn to control yourself in many ways so you can live by God's rules and do the things He wants you to do. Deer live in the forest. Do you know anything else that lives there? Try looking through some magazines. As you find pictures of what you might find in the forest, cut them out. Then paste them onto a piece of construction paper or cardboard so you can make your own picture of a forest. Maybe you'll even find some baby deer to put in your picture! Below is a picture of Natalie and her daddy with the baby fawn for you to finish coloring."

Guidance

God guides me.

He will be our guide even to the end.

~ Psalm 48:14

Now What?

"Dig deeper," said Mommy as Anna scooped dirt out of the hole with her small shovel. "If we're going to plant these potatoes, the hole needs to be a lot deeper."

Anna pushed and stabbed at the dirt, but it was too hard. "I need help," she said.

Mommy put her hand over Anna's, and together they pushed the shovel through the hard dirt. Anna scooped out the soil, making the hole bigger.

"Now what?" asked Anna, as she set down her shovel.

"Now get the wooden stake so we can mark where we have these planted," said Mommy. Anna got the wooden stake, and Mommy pushed it into the ground.

"Now what?" asked Anna again.

"We can plant the potatoes now," said Mommy, "and then we'll be all done."

Mommy guided Anna to plant the potatoes. In the same way, God guides you to do the right things in your life. When you ask, "Now what?" the words in the Bible teach you how to live. When you need to ask God for some extra help, you can always pray to Him.

Your Turn

1. Does your mommy ever guide you? How?

_____

_____

2. How does God guide you?

_____

_____

Prayer

Thank You, God, for guiding me in all that I do. Amen.

Guiding Maze

Read this to your child: "God guides you in all that you do. Here's a maze for you to do. Let the signs guide you to the end."

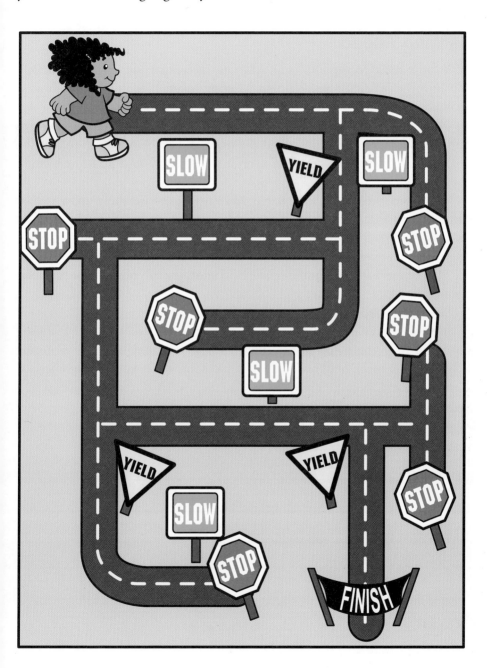

Planning Ahead

God wants me to plan ahead to do more for Him.

Many are the plans in a man's heart.

~ Proverbs 19:21

Planting Ahead

"A little more to the left," said Mommy as Jennifer dropped the daffodil bulb into the hole. She was helping Mommy plant their new bulbs around the mailbox.

"Why are we doing this now?" asked Jennifer. She knew that winter was coming. All the leaves had fallen off the trees, and her hands were cold as she held the bulbs. Jennifer knew that soon it would snow, and no flowers could grow through the snow.

"We plant these now," answered Mommy, "because these are a special kind of flower that need to be in the cold ground for a long time before they can bloom. Only if we plant them now can we see them bloom in the spring when winter is over."

"Right here?" asked Jennifer as she held another bulb over one of the holes Mommy had dug.

"Yes," answered Mommy, "that's perfect."

Some things work better if you plan for them ahead of time. Planning ahead will help you to be in the right place at the right time. By planning ahead, you can make better use of your time. God wants you to plan ahead as often as you can, because then you can do more with all that He gives you.

Your Turn

1. How do you plan ahead?

_____

_____

2. Why does God want you to plan ahead?

_____

_____

Prayer

God, please help me to plan ahead as much as possible so I can make the best use of all that You have given me. Amen.

Things to Plan For

Read this to your child: "Planning ahead helps you to make the most of all that God gives you. Here are some things for which you need to plan ahead. Circle the things in each picture that you help plan."

Resistance
God wants me to have good behavior.

Resist the devil, and he will flee from you.
~ James 4:7

Resisting Evil

"Take just one piece," said the store clerk to the children.

Sydney was shopping with her Mommy and sisters in the store, and the clerk had a dish of candy she was offering them. "I always like to have candy for the children," the clerk explained.

Sydney looked carefully at the dish of candy. There were so many kinds to choose from that it was very hard to pick just one. She wanted to be good and take only one, but she really wanted the red one and the purple one.

Sydney reached out and took the red piece of candy, but stopped before pulling her hand back. She heard the lady say again, "Just one piece."

As Sydney held the red piece of candy in her hand, she told herself that God would want her to do the right thing. Pulling her hand back, she looked up at the lady and said, "Thank you" before popping the candy into her mouth.

Resistance, like most things, can be used for good or bad. God wants you to resist bad behavior. Sydney resisted the urge to take an extra piece of candy. She knew that even though she wanted another one, it wasn't the right thing to do. Ask God to help you resist doing bad things.

Your Turn

1. Is resisting a good thing or a bad thing to do?

_____

_____

2. When was the last time you resisted doing something bad?

_____

_____

Prayer

God, please help me to resist bad behavior. Amen

Resisting Coins

Read this to your child: "God wants you to resist bad things. A coin won't easily stand on edge by itself, but if you spin it, it will (until it slows down). Try it. When the coin is spinning, it resists any change in the way it is spinning."

Discovery

God made a world for me to discover.

God saw all that he had made, and it was very good.

~ Genesis 1:31

Taylor's Apples

Taylor looked at the sliced apples on her plate. Mommy had cut them up for her earlier, but Taylor had decided to watch TV before sitting down to eat.

Now her apples looked all brown and yucky.

"These apples are spoiled," said Taylor.

"No, they're not," answered Mommy, "you just let them set for too long before eating them."

"What do you mean?" Taylor asked.

Mommy picked up the slices on the top of the dish. "Look," she said, "see how the apples that were covered are still white? That's because the air couldn't get to them. The apples on top were in the air, so they turned brown."

"But they're yucky now," said Taylor, scrunching up her nose.

"No," said Mommy, "they're just brown from the air. There's nothing wrong with them."

God made an amazing world for you to live in! There are many things to learn and discover. If you pay attention to what is happening around you, you will discover, as Taylor did, some of the wonderful ways God made the world to work.

Your Turn

1. What is something you have discovered?

_____

_____

2. Who made the world?

_____

_____

Prayer

God, thank You for making such an amazing world for me to discover. Amen.

Apple Osmosis

Read this to your child: "God made an amazing world for you to discover. Here's something else you can discover about the world using apples. Slice an apple in half. Sprinkle salt on one piece. Wait a few minutes. Now look at the salted apple. It should look like it's wet. Look at the other piece. It should look like it's drying and it should be stiffer. This reaction is due to 'osmosis.' Here's a picture for you to finish coloring of Taylor eating her apple."

Ingenuity

God gives me ingenuity to do good things.

God gave knowledge and understanding of all kinds.

~ Daniel 1:17

Too Many Toys

"There's too many toys!" Elizabeth cried. "I can't do it."

"You brought the toys downstairs, so you can take them back up the stairs," said Mommy.

Elizabeth knew the house rule that if she brought toys downstairs from her room she had to take them back up at the end of the day. She had brought down a lot of toys that day. Now it seemed like an impossible job to carry them all back up.

"How can I take all these toys back upstairs by myself?" asked Elizabeth.

"Just carry a couple at a time," Mommy said.

"But that will take forever!" Elizabeth cried.

Elizabeth started to pick up two of her toys and then stopped when she saw her pink blanket on the floor. Suddenly she had a great idea. Spreading her blanket out on the floor, she piled all of her toys onto the center of it. Then she carefully folded up the corners and dragged the blanket (with all the toys inside) up the stairs. In one trip she finished her job!

Elizabeth thought of a way to make her job easier. This is called "ingenuity." In the same way, God wants you to do your best to think of ways to help people and make the world a better place. God gives you ingenuity.

Your Turn

1. How did Elizabeth get all her toys back upstairs with only one trip?

_____

_____

2. Have you ever thought of a way to do something in an easier way?

_____

_____

Prayer

Thank You, God, for making me so smart that I can think of better ways to do things. Help me to use my ingenuity. Amen.

Musical Grass

Read this to your child: "God wants you to do your best to think of new things that will make the world a better place. That's why He gave you a brain! With a little ingenuity, you should be able to do this activity quite well. Just hold a blade of grass (a wider blade works well) between your thumbs and blow against it. The vibration of the grass back and forth creates the sound you hear. Here's a picture of Elizabeth making sounds with grass. You can finish coloring it."

I Can Learn About Feelings

Surprises

God helps me with good and bad surprises.

In all things God works for the good.

~ Romans 8:28

Easter Surprises

The children in the Jones family got a special surprise for Easter. Their grandma and grandpa brought them each a fuzzy baby bunny. One was white, and he was named "Tibblets." The other was brown and named "Tisa."

They were very nice bunnies until the day after Easter. Tibblets didn't want to go back into his cage. He ran under the shelves in Daddy's garage and wouldn't come out. Mommy tried everything she could think of, but nothing worked. Tibblets just wouldn't come out.

As Mommy reached for Tibblets, little Sarah walked up. "It's a mouse," she said.

"It's not a mouse," answered Mommy, not looking up. "It's a rabbit."

"It's a mouse, a mouse!" Sarah said again as she stood behind Mommy.

Mommy finally stopped reaching for Tibblets and turned to look behind her. There stood Sarah, holding a tiny gray field mouse by its back legs. When Mommy screamed, Sarah dropped the mouse and started to cry. Mommy was so surprised to see Sarah holding a mouse that she screamed, and Sarah was so surprised to hear Mommy scream that she started to cry.

God gives you many different kinds of surprises. The bunnies were a good surprise, but the mouse was a bad one. You can be thankful for the good surprises in your life, and count on God to help you with the bad ones.

Your Turn

1. Why did Mommy think Sarah was talking about the bunny?

_____

_____

2. Can you remember the last time you were surprised? Was it good or bad?

_____

_____

Prayer

Thank You, God, for all the good surprises in life, and thank You also for helping with the bad ones. Amen.

Good and Bad Surprises

Read this to your child: "God gives you many different kinds of surprises. Here are some surprises. Which ones do you think are good, and which are bad? Can you think of anything good about the bad surprises? Talk to Mommy or Daddy about them."

Amazement

I am amazed at God's love.

You gave me life and showed me kindness.

~ Job 10:12

Expected Surprises

"Surprise!" Ellie called as she walked into the house, slamming the front door behind her. "I have a surprise for you, Mommy."

"What is it?" asked Mommy, although she already knew the answer. Every day when Ellie got home from Kindergarten she brought the mail in with her.

Ellie put the mail in her backpack. Every time she did that she also picked up some weeds or sticks–anything she thought was pretty–to put in her backpack, too. These were all special surprises for Mommy.

Mommy picked the weeds and sticks out of Ellie's backpack. She didn't mind that she already knew what the "surprise" was, or even that it was weeds and sticks. What mattered to Mommy was that Ellie had wanted to do something nice for her, and that made Mommy feel loved.

As you learn about the Bible you will find many things that amaze you. There are stories about how Jesus performed miracles, and how He did so much to help and teach us. It's amazing that God could love us all so much that He even died for our sins.

Amazing events can be big or little, pretty or plain–it doesn't really matter. What matters is that when you see something amazing, or do something to surprise someone, it should be out of love and kindness.

Your Turn

1. Why do you think Ellie wanted to surprise her mommy?

   kind and loveing

2. What have you learned about Jesus or the Bible that amazed you?

   he risen people

Prayer

Thank You, Jesus, for all the wonderful surprises of Your love. Amen.

Good and Bad Surprises

Read this to your child: "God amazes us in many ways. In the Bible, Jesus did many miracles that amazed a lot of people. It's also amazing how much God loves us—more than anyone else! Here are some surprises. Which one would you find good and which, if any, would you find bad? Circle the good one(s), then finish coloring the pictures."

Wonder

God created a world full of beautiful, wonderful things.

Sing to him, sing praise to him; tell of all his wonderful acts.
~ Psalm 105:2

Wonder-ful Butterflies

Lauren loved going to the park, especially the park that had a greenhouse in it. The greenhouse was a building with glass walls and lots of plants. Lauren liked walking around inside the greenhouse and seeing all the different kinds of plants, but most of all she loved butterflies–and today the greenhouse had hatched many butterflies.

Lauren was surprised when she stepped through the door and saw more butterflies than she had ever seen before. Red, orange and yellow butterflies flew past her. Blue, soft wings brushed by her as Lauren carefully walked forward. When she held out her hand, a big, orange and black butterfly landed on her finger for a moment before flying away again. Mommy even took a picture as a butterfly sat on Lauren's head, softly fluttering its wings.

The world is full of wonderful, beautiful things. God made it that way. Lauren was surprised by the beauty of the butterflies. She felt wonder at seeing so many beautiful things all in one place. You should always feel that wonder when you look at the world that God created for you.

Your Turn

1. Do you like butterflies? Why or why not?

_____

_____

2. What do you like best about God's creation?

_____

_____

Prayer

Thank You, God, for making such a beautiful world filled with so many wonderful things. Amen.

Butterfly Fun

Read this to your child: "Butterflies are just one of the many wonderful things in this world that God made for you to enjoy. Here is a way you can make your very own butterfly (or you can just color the one below). Lay a piece of paper over the outline, then cut out your picture and color it. If you attach a string, you can even 'fly' your butterfly around the house."

Excitement

God fills my world with excitement.

In frenzied excitement…he cannot stand still.
~ Job 39:24

The Air Show

When Bethany heard the low, rumbling sound she wondered what it was. What could be making that sound? Suddenly, she figured it out. The sound was just like what she heard when Daddy took her to an air show. Daddy had taken her to a big field where they sat on a blanket and munched on popcorn as huge planes flew over them. It was great fun, and now Bethany could hear sounds just like those she had heard before.

Bethany was so excited to think that right over her house there was another air show! "Let's go outside," Bethany shouted to the other kids. "Let's go to the air show!"

Bethany and all the children ran outside to watch the plane. When the pilot saw them, he flew his plane back and forth over the house as the kids jumped up and down screaming and waving their arms. It was the most fun and excitement Bethany had all day.

God fills your world with fun, exciting things: planes that fly through the air, race cars that drive very fast, hot air balloons that float high above the ground…so many things that can make you smile and giggle. He has given you many things to make you happy!

Your Turn

1. What kinds of things make you smile and giggle?

_____

_____

2. What has God given you that makes you happy?

_____

_____

Prayer

Thank You, God, for all the exciting things in the world. Amen.

Paper Airplane

Read this to your child: "God has given you so many exciting things! Bethany loved watching the airplanes. Here's a way you can make your own airplane with just a simple piece of paper. Fold it as shown below."

Step 1

Fold the paper edges toward each other until they meet, as shown.

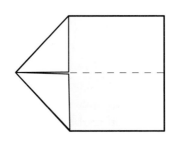

Step 2

Fold the edges toward each other again until they meet. You will now have an even narrower point.

Step 3

Fold the paper lengthwise down the middle. This time you are not folding the sides toward each other but rather away from each other.

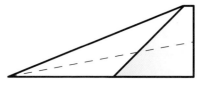

Step 4

Make one last fold on each side, bringing the wing on each side down, as shown.

Fear

I can pray when I am afraid.

So do not fear...I will strengthen you and help you.

~ Isaiah 41:10

Ghost Cow

"Moo, moo," Mommy heard from the next room. A moment later Holly came walking up with a blanket over her head.

"Oh, my," said Mommy. "I think a ghost cow is in the house."

"I'm not a ghost cow," said Holly. "I'm very scary." Holly walked around the room. She bumped into the wall and chair because she couldn't see very well with the blanket over her head!

"Moo, moo," Holly called again. She wanted to play with Mommy by pretending to be scary, but Mommy was laughing!

"Oh," said Mommy between giggles, "I'm very scared." Holly laughed then, too, and went to see who else she could scare in the house.

There are many scary things in the world, but sometimes what seems scary isn't really so bad. Holly thought she was being very scary, but she wasn't. Holly was more silly than scary.

The world can be that way too. God made the world full of many different kinds of things–and they aren't always as scary as they seem to be. Sometimes when you take a closer look at what scares you, you may find that it's not so scary after all. But if you are afraid, you know you can always pray to God for help.

Your Turn

1. Have you ever thought something was scary but then found out it was silly? What was it?

_____

_____

2. What can you do when you are afraid? (Pray.)

_____

_____

Prayer

God, please help me to remember that things are not always what they seem to be. Help me not to be afraid. Amen.

Scary Things

Read this to your child: "God made everything, including things that sometimes seem scary. What are you afraid of? Here are some pictures of things that make some people feel afraid. Circle the ones that scare you, then put an "X" through the ones that don't. There's an empty box at the bottom of the page for you to draw what scares you. Talk to your mommy or daddy about why that scares you, then pray and ask God to help take away your fears."

Love

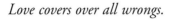

God's love makes me feel better.

Love covers over all wrongs.

~ Proverbs 10:12

The Best Medicine

"Ow," cried Paige as tears began running down her cheeks. She had bumped her arm against the corner of the TV and hurt herself. Now she was standing next to the TV feeling very sad and alone, and not knowing what to do.

"Ow," Paige yelled again. "It hurts, it hurts."

"Come here," called Mommy. "Let me see your boo-boo and I'll make it better."

Paige ran to Mommy and pointed to where her arm hurt. The spot on her arm was very red and sore. "I need medicine," said Paige.

"I've got just the right kind of medicine for you," said Mommy as she hugged Paige close and kissed her boo-boo. "I'm giving you the best medicine of all…love."

Paige looked down at where Mommy had kissed her boo-boo. It was still red and sore, but Paige did feel a little better. She wasn't crying anymore, and she even had a tiny smile on her face.

Even though Mommy's kiss couldn't make Paige's boo-boo go away, it still made Paige feel better. That's because love is the strongest feeling that there is. Mommy made Paige feel better, just like God's love makes you feel each and every day. His love for you saves you from your sins, and He keeps loving you no matter what.

Your Turn

1. What did Paige's mommy do to make her feel better?

_____

_____

2. What does God do to help you?

_____

_____

Prayer

God, thank You for loving me, and for helping me to love others. Amen.

Homemade Envelope

Read this to your child: "There are many different ways to show love. God gives you His love every day. You can give love with this envelope you make yourself. Just follow the directions, and you'll see."

What You Need

square piece of paper

ribbon or string

crayons

What to Do

1. Color the square piece of paper any way you like.
2. Flip over the paper so your pretty picture is on the bottom.
3. Place a small gift (a small piece of candy works well) in the center.
4. Lift up each corner toward the center, wrap a string or ribbon around the four sections of paper and tie.
5. You now have a pretty package all ready to given to someone you love!

Contentment

God's love makes me content.

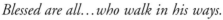

Blessed are all…who walk in his ways.

~ Psalm 128:1

The Moon and the Stars

Mommy loved to snuggle with all of her children, and that was a good thing, because they all loved to snuggle with her, too.

One day as Mommy snuggled baby Bianca tight, big sister Danielle overheard Mommy say, "Holding you is like holding the moon and the stars."

"What do you mean, Mommy?" asked Danielle. "Why is holding Bianca like holding the moon and the stars?"

"Because holding my children is such a wonderful feeling, it's like nothing on this earth."

Danielle thought about what Mommy had said. Snuggling was a wonderful thing, she decided, but why? What was it about snuggling with Mommy that felt so good?

When you snuggle with your mommy or daddy, how do you feel? You probably feel content. That's what you feel when you're safe, warm and relaxed.

That's also how thinking about God can make you feel. Knowing that God is always with you, holding you close (even though you can't see Him) and loving you, can give you a feeling of contentment—just like snuggling.

Your Turn

1. How does snuggling make you feel?

_____

_____

2. How does God's love make you feel?

_____

_____

Prayer

God, thank You for always holding me close, even though I can't see you. Amen.

Door Snuggler

Read this to your child: "Some of the most wonderful things that God gives you are feelings like love, contentment and happiness. Here's something you can make yourself that can 'snuggle' up to the door and keep it from closing on you. Just have Mommy or Daddy save an empty soda or detergent bottle. Wash it out and then fill it with dirt, small rocks or sand. Peel off any labels the bottle has on it. Then glue or tape on a face that you've cut out of an old magazine. Now you can color, paint, or paste more pictures on your bottle, or decorate it any way you wish."

Confidence

God believes in me.

It is better to take refuge in the Lord than to trust in man.

~ Psalm 118:8

Look at Me!

"Look at me, everyone," called Kara as she stood on top of a chair in the living room.

Tonight was the birthday party for her little sister, but she had just gotten a present herself from her mommy.

"I just got a new book," Kara said to the birthday guests, "and anyone who wants to hear some silly jokes should meet me in the corner of the room." Kara was just learning to read. She knew that she wouldn't know all the words in the joke book, but she was sure that if she tried her best, she could figure out the jokes well enough to read them to everyone else.

The first jokes in the book were hard to read. They had some very big words that Kara had never seen before, but Kara didn't let that stop her. She just filled in the words that she thought should be there, and in some cases, even made up her own jokes. Everyone laughed at Kara's jokes, but more importantly, everyone loved the fact that Kara was reading to them.

Kara had confidence. She believed in herself and her ability to read. Even when she didn't know a word, she didn't let that stop her. God wants you to be like that. He wants you to believe in yourself, because He believes in you, too. You can do almost anything you really want to do!

Your Turn

1. Are you good at reading as Kara is? What are you good at?

_____

_____

2. What does God help you to do?

_____

_____

Prayer

Thank You, God, for believing in me. I'll try hard to believe in me, too. Amen.

Book Maze

Read this to your child: "You can do anything you really want to do because God believes in you, and you should believe in you, too. Here's something you can do if you just believe in yourself. Find your way through the maze of books. Don't give up—you can do it!"

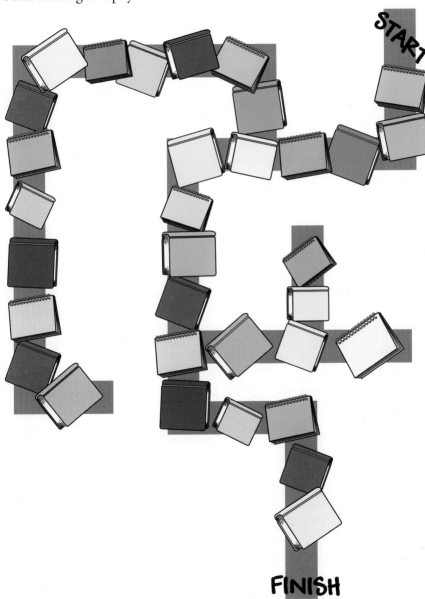

Appreciation

I should appreciate what God gives me.

Let him go home…and someone else enjoy it.

~ Deuteronomy 20:6

Where's My Kangaroo?

Erin liked the paper kangaroo she made. Her library had given her the cut-out pieces, and she had carefully put them together to make a beautiful kangaroo. When she was done, Erin even colored her kangaroo with many different crayons just to make it extra pretty.

Mommy thought Erin's kangaroo was so special that she taped it on the kitchen wall and left it there for the entire summer. Mommy would ask Erin about the kangaroo from time to time, but Erin never seemed to be very interested in it. In fact, Erin never said anything about her kangaroo. Mommy started to think that Erin didn't care about her kangaroo very much, so she decided one day to take it down. When Erin's sister, Faith, made a turkey picture, Mommy took down the kangaroo and put up the turkey in its place.

Five minutes after the turkey had gone up, Erin walked into the kitchen and cried, "Where's my kangaroo?"

Erin hadn't appreciated that Mommy had put her kangaroo up on the wall. She thought it would just always be there, but once it was gone, Erin realized how much she really did care about her paper kangaroo.

God gives you many wonderful things and loving people in your life. You should always appreciate what He has given you.

Your Turn

1. Why do you think Erin seemed not to care about her kangaroo until it was gone?

_____

_____

2. How do you appreciate all that you have?

_____

_____

Prayer

Thank You, God, for everything and everyone You have given me. I will try my best to never take anything for granted. Amen.

Face Hand

Read this to your child: "You should appreciate everything that God has given you, including your hands! Here's something you can do with your hands that's lots of fun. Use a watercolor marker to draw a face on your hand like the one shown below. You can put some yarn on top of your hand for hair, or even some bunched-up tissue works well. See if you can make your hand 'talk'!"

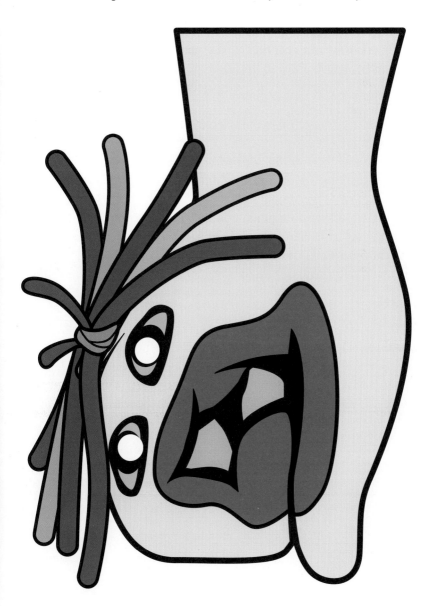

Happiness

Happiness comes from God.

To the man who pleases him, God gives…happiness.

~ Ecclesiastes 2:26

Nothing in There?

Daddy had brought in pumpkins from the garden. Gabrielle and Samantha loved pumpkin pie, and Mommy said she'd make one if they cleaned out the pumpkins. As they worked to scoop out the insides, Gabrielle had an idea. "Let's draw faces on these," she said.

Gabrielle and Samantha ran to get the big, black markers, and soon they were drawing on the outside of the pumpkins. When they were done, they stood back to admire their work.

Gabrielle looked at Samantha's pumpkin. "Why is he smiling?" she asked. "He only has two teeth."

"Happiness doesn't have to do with what you have or who you know…or even how many teeth you have," said Mommy. "Happiness has to do with what's inside you."

Happiness is not about how much you have, or how you look. Happiness comes from who you are inside. A new toy or pretty dress may make you happy for a little while, but that's not lasting. True happiness comes from the love of God that fills you, and the goodness and beauty that is who you are inside.

Your Turn

1. Does happiness have to do with what you have or how you look?

_____

_____

2. What makes you happy?

_____

_____

Prayer

Thank You, God, for Your love and all the goodness that it brings about in the world, and in me. Amen.

Pumpkin Equation

Read this to your child: "Happiness comes from God's love and all the goodness that you have inside. Here are three groups of pumpkins. Count how many there are in each group, then circle the correct number."

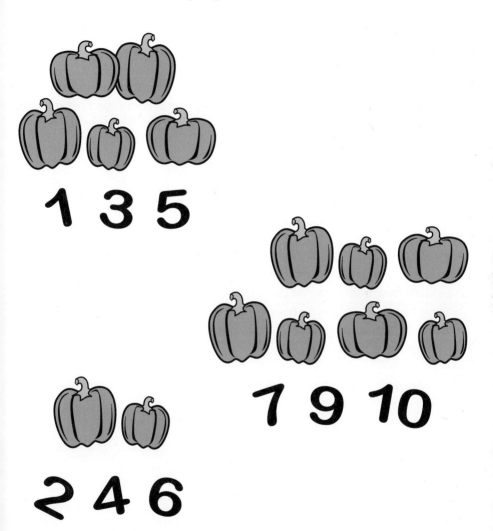

1 3 5

7 9 10

2 4 6

Worry

Instead of worrying, I should trust in God.

The mind controlled by the Spirit is life and peace.

~ Romans 8:6

Worrying Over Nothing

The roar of the lawn mower was so loud that Ellen could hear it inside the house. She ran to the window and looked out to see Daddy riding on the mower in the back yard.

"Oh, no," Ellen cried, "he'll scare the bunnies! Stop him, Mommy, stop him!"

"It's okay," said Mommy. "Daddy won't go too close to the bunny hutch with the mower. He knows about the bunnies. He won't scare them."

"But what if he does?" Ellen asked, tears forming in her eyes.

"He won't," said Mommy. "As I said, Daddy would never scare your bunnies."

"But why does he have to mow the lawn?" Ellen cried.

"He has to mow the lawn," Mommy answered. "But it won't take long."

Ellen kept worrying about the bunnies even though she knew deep down that her daddy would never do anything to scare her bunnies. Mowing the lawn wasn't something that she could change either. The lawn had to be mowed. Worrying about the bunnies didn't make a lot of sense.

God doesn't want you to worry about things that you can't change. Worrying needlessly can only hurt you and keep you from being the best that you can be. Instead of worrying, you should put your trust in God, just as Ellen should have trusted her daddy to not hurt her bunnies.

Your Turn

1. Did it make sense for Ellen to be worried? Why, or why not?

_____

_____

2. Do you ever worry about things that make no sense?

_____

_____

Prayer

God, please help me to put my trust in You and not to worry about things that I can't change or that don't make sense. Amen.

Things to Worry Over

Read this to your child: "God doesn't want you to worry over things you can't change or that don't make any sense. You should put your trust in Him instead. Here are some things that people sometimes worry about. Which ones worry you? Draw a line from each picture to the face that shows how you feel about it."

I Can Know God

Reading

Reading helps me to learn about God.

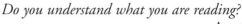

Do you understand what you are reading?

~ Acts 8:30

Reading Pictures

"Will you read this bird story with me?" asked Mackenzie.

Mackenzie loved books that had pictures instead of words so she could "read" along with Mommy. The one she held in her lap was one of her favorites.

"Okay, honey," said Mommy, as she snuggled beside Mackenzie on the couch. Mommy loved to read with Mackenzie.

As Mommy began to read, Mackenzie saw the story's pictures in her mind. When real pictures came along, she "read" them to Mommy. Mackenzie and Mommy read the whole story together. Mackenzie couldn't wait until she would be able to read the words all by herself someday!

Mackenzie loved reading even though she couldn't read words yet. God likes for you to read, because that way you will learn to read the Bible and find out more about Him. The Bible tells how you should live your life.

But even if you cannot read yet, there are ways to learn about God. You can listen in church, have Mommy or Daddy read you Bible stories, or even look at the pictures you find in your books about God. All of those things will help you to learn about God until you're old enough to read the Bible all by yourself.

1. How did Mackenzie "read" her book?

_____

_____

2. Do you have any books that you can read just by looking at the pictures?

_____

_____

Prayer

God, please help me learn to read, so that I can read the Bible and learn more about You. Amen.

Picture Reading

Read this to your child: "God wants you to learn to read so you can read the Bible and learn all about Him. Here's a story like Mackenzie read with her mommy. Your mommy or daddy can read the words, and you can read the pictures. When you're done with this story, you can make up your own story. It's fun!"

The blue   through the .

It was looking to if it could find a place to

rest. Suddenly, the blue saw a beautiful ,

so it down and sat on its . It was a perfect

spot to rest. From its  high in the , the

 could 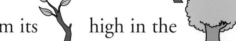 many wonderful things. The

 could a hunting for 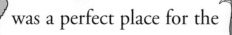,

and a slithering through the . It could even

see some small crawling across a . Yes,

the was a perfect place for the to rest,

and the was very .

Baptism

Baptism is a promise to God.

This water symbolizes baptism.

~ 1 Peter 3:21

Baptism Day

It was a very special day. Hailey's older sister, Katherine, was going to be baptized. Before they left for the church service, their mommy cleaned the house, and set out the special cake she had made for Katherine's baptism party.

Hailey skipped happily through the house in her fancy church dress and shiny black shoes. She loved to dress up, and couldn't wait until the service was over so the party could start.

As Hailey bounced into the kitchen, she looked at the beautiful white cake on the kitchen counter. "Mmm" she hummed as she licked her lips.

"Mommy," Hailey asked, "why do we have a special cake when it isn't even anyone's birthday?"

Mommy smiled and answered, "Because today is like a birthday, and it's even more important."

"More important than a birthday?!" Hailey said with surprise.

"Yes, honey," Mommy continued, "because today Katherine will show that she is a member of God's family when she is baptized."

Baptism is a very special day—even more special than your birthday. You should remember your baptism as one of the most important days in your life, and celebrate it always.

Your Turn

1. Why is baptism so important?

_____

_____

2. Ask your mommy and daddy to tell you about their baptisms. Do you think you might like to be baptized some day?

_____

_____

Prayer

Dear God, thank You for the beautiful gift of baptism, when I can show everyone that I want to follow You. Amen.

Baptism Symbols

Read this to your child: "Baptism is very special. It is a way for you to show everyone that You want to follow God. Here are some things you might see at a baptism. Talk about them with your mommy or daddy. Which ones have you seen before? What do you think each of them is used for? Finish coloring the pictures."

Thanks

I should thank God for all I have.

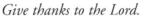

Give thanks to the Lord.

~ 1 Chronicles 16:8

Giving Thanks

"Thanksgiving is about Pilgrims and Indians eating dinner together," said Alyssa with a smile. "We learned all about it in Sunday school."

"Yes, that's true," said Mommy, "but that's not what Thanksgiving is all about."

"Yes it is," insisted Alyssa. "It's about Pilgrims eating dinner."

"Well," answered Mommy, "Pilgrims did eat dinner with the Indians on the very first Thanksgiving, but there was a very special reason for the dinner."

"What was that?" asked Alyssa.

"Giving thanks," said Mommy. "The Pilgrims were so thankful for all that they had, that they had a special meal with the Indians to thank God. Each year, we celebrate Thanksgiving by having a dinner like the Pilgrims did, to thank God for all that He has given us."

Thanking God is an important thing for you to do. He has given you everything you have. He even died for your sins. You should thank Him every day, but especially on Thanksgiving, the special day that is set aside just for thanking God.

Your Turn

1. What is Thanksgiving really about?

_____

_____

2. How do you and your family celebrate Thanksgiving?

_____

_____

Prayer

Dear God, thank You for everything that You have given me. Amen.

Thank You, Jesus, Card

Read this to your child: "When you get a gift from someone, do you ever send a thank-you card? Some people do that. Make a thank-you card to Jesus for all He gives you. Fold a piece of paper into fourths so it looks like a card. Ask your mommy or daddy to help you write all of the things for which you are thankful. Instead of mailing your card, keep it by your bed so when you say your nighttime prayers it will remind you of all that Jesus has given you. Some of the things you could put on your list are drawn below."

Prayer

I can pray to God.

God has surely listened and heard my voice in prayer.
~ Psalm 66:19

The Right Prayer

"That's not part of the prayer," said Kenny. His little sister, Lucy, was saying her bedtime prayers, and at the end she always added, "I love You very, very, very much," and then she would say what she was thankful for that day.

"She's messing up the prayer," Kenny said to Mommy. "Tell her how to do it right."

"She is doing it right," answered Mommy. "Lucy says the same prayer that you do, but then she likes to add something special at the end–something that is just from her to God."

"Can I do that, too?" asked Kenny.

"Sure," said Mommy. "Just tell God how you feel about Him, and then think about what you liked the most today and thank Him for that. That's what Lucy does."

Kenny listened carefully to Lucy the next time she said her prayers. When she reached the end of her prayer, she added, "I love you very, very, very much, God. Thank You especially today for making it sunny so I could play outside."

I can do that, thought Kenny, and from then on he did.

There's nothing wrong with saying what you feel inside when you pray to God. God loves to hear you talk to Him, whether it's a prayer that you've been taught, or just saying that you love Him.

Your Turn

1. What did Lucy like to add at the end of her prayer?

_____

_____

2. Do you say anything special (just from you) in your prayers at night?

_____

_____

Prayer

Thank You, God, for listening to me when I pray. I know You love me, and I'm glad You want to hear what I have to say. Amen.

126

Special Prayers

Read this to your child: "God loves to hear you pray. He likes to hear what you're thinking and feeling and what you liked about your day. Lucy liked to add something special to her regular prayer each night. You can do that, too. Have your mommy or daddy help you fill in the lines below. When you're done, you can finish coloring the picture of Lucy praying."

Thank You, God, for _____.

My favorite thing about today was _____.

Please take special care of _____.

When I think about You I feel _____.

Trinity

God can be called by more than one name.

In the name of the Father and of the Son and of the Holy Spirit.
~ Matthew 28:19

Jesus, God and the Ghost

Mommy, Daddy, Stephanie and baby Jamie sat down in the church pew for the service. As Mommy helped everyone take off their coats and hats, she saw that Stephanie was already fidgeting and looking for something to do.

"You'd better be good," Mommy whispered in Stephanie's ear, "because everybody's watching you. Mommy is watching you, Daddy is watching you, baby Jamie is watching you and God is watching you."

"What about Jesus?" Stephanie asked. "Is He watching me, too? And what about the Holy Ghost? Is He watching me, too?"

Mommy smiled at Stephanie. She was proud of Stephanie for remembering that God could be called by more than one name. "Yes, honey," Mommy answered as she stroked Stephanie's long hair, "Jesus and the Holy Ghost are watching you, too."

God can be called by more than one name. You may sometimes hear people say "Trinity" or "Father, Son and Holy Ghost." Those are all ways to talk about God or Jesus. No matter what God is called, He is with you, loving you and watching over you always.

Your Turn

1. What names can you call God?

_____

_____

2. What name is your favorite for God?

_____

_____

Prayer

God, please help me to remember that no matter what name You are called, You are still my God. Amen.

Worshiping Jesus

Read this to your child: "God is the same no matter what name you call Him. Here's a picture of Stephanie in church (turn the book sideways to see it correctly). Finish coloring the picture."

Constancy

Jesus is always the same.

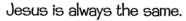

Jesus Christ is the same yesterday and today and forever.

~ Hebrews 13:18

Things

"Tony, get my thing," said Shannon.

"What thing?" asked Tony, her older brother.

"My thing!" Shannon screamed.

"Mommy," Tony said. "Shannon calls everything her 'thing.' Why does she do that?"

"Shannon is still very little," answered Mommy, "and it's difficult for her to say some words, so she says 'thing' because it's easier."

"Well, I don't like it," said Tony. "It bugs me. She should know that everything is different. Everything has its own name."

"She does," said Mommy. "When she wants her blankie or her cup, she knows what they really are. She just doesn't think that the name is all that important. All that's important is what those things are."

You can call something by many different names, but that doesn't change what it is. Shannon called everything her "thing," but that didn't change what it was. In the same way, no matter what you hear Jesus called, He's still Jesus. Some people say "God" and some say "Lord" but that's still Jesus. Jesus is always the same, just as He always cares for you and loves you.

Your Turn

1. Why did Shannon call everything her "thing"?

_____

_____

2. Who is always the same no matter what name you use?

_____

_____

Prayer

Thank You, Jesus, for always being You, no matter what I hear You called. Thank You for always taking care of me and loving me. Amen.

Finger Puppets

Read this to your child: "It doesn't matter what name something is called, it's still the same thing. In the same way, Jesus is always the same, and He always loves you. Here's an activity where you can make puppets and call them whatever names you like. Cut some pieces of paper into strips (3" x 4" works well). Construction paper works best. Draw a picture as shown. Now wrap the paper around your finger and secure it with tape. Do this on each finger, and you'll have a whole collection of finger puppets! What names will you use?"

Christmas

Jesus is more important than Santa.

The gift of God is eternal life in Christ Jesus.

~ Romans 6:23

Special Gifts

As Megan was lying in her bed, she thought about her birthday that day. The whole day had been just for her, with a fun dinner, fancy cake and special gifts. One of her favorite gifts was a watch that her Aunt Laura had sent her. Even though Aunt Laura lived far away, she never forgot to send a gift for Megan on her birthday.

As Mommy tucked in Megan for the night and started to leave the room, Megan said, "Mommy, would you e-mail Aunt Laura and tell her thank you for the gifts?"

"Sure, honey," Mommy answered. "I'll do that first thing in the morning."

"Aunt Laura's kind of like my special Santa," Megan added.

"Why is that?" Mommy asked.

"Because I never see her, but she sends me gifts that are only for me."

Megan said that Aunt Laura was like her "special Santa," but do you know who is like your special Santa? Jesus is far more special than Santa could ever be, and He has given you a much better gift. His gift to you is everlasting life and a love that never ends. It's fun to think about Santa at Christmas time, but don't forget the most important and best gift of all is Jesus.

Your Turn

1. Why did Megan say Aunt Laura was like her special Santa?

_____

_____

2. Why is Jesus like your special Santa?

_____

_____

Prayer

Thank You for Jesus, the best gift of all. Please help me to remember that Jesus is the most important person at Christmas, not Santa. Amen.

Present Sizes

Read this to your child: "Jesus is the most important person at Christmas, not Santa. Jesus' gifts are the best of all! Here are some gifts. Can you choose which is the biggest, the smallest, and the one in-between? Finish coloring the one that is your favorite."

Creation

God made the world and everything in it.

God created the heavens and the earth.

~ Genesis 1:1

Bria's Creation

"Look what I made," said Bria as she held up a clay snowman she had made. She was very proud of it.

"That's beautiful," said Mommy with a smile. "I think that's the best clay snowman I've ever seen!"

"It was hard," said Bria, "and it took me a long time."

"Do you think you could have made the snowman without any clay?" Mommy asked.

"Without any clay?" Bria said. "How could I do that?"

"Just think how God made everything, and He didn't even have any clay to start out with. He didn't have anything at all."

"I don't understand," said Bria. "I made my snowman out of clay, but it was hard. I don't see how God could make a whole world with no clay or paint or anything. If I couldn't do it, and you couldn't even do it, then how could He?"

God made the world and everything in it. He started with nothing at all, and made everything from dirt and rocks to animals and people. It's hard to imagine how He could do it, but He did.

Your Turn

1. Could Bria have made her snowman without clay?

_____

_____

2. Did God make everything? How did He do it?

_____

_____

Prayer

Thank You, God, for making the world and everything in it. Amen.

Making Things

Read this to your child: "God made the whole world and everything in it. Draw a line from the supplies on the left to what they make on the right. You can finish coloring the pictures when you're done."

Faith

Faith in God makes life easier.

I have faith in God that it will happen just as he told me.

~ Acts 27:25

Hannah's Tests

Hannah sat in the car and stared out the window in front of her. She was on the way to the doctor for some tests. She could see her hands shaking…and so could Mommy.

"Are you scared?" Mommy asked.

"Just a little," Hannah answered. "I don't want it to hurt."

"It might hurt a little," Mommy said, "but not a lot, and it'll be over before you know it."

"But what if it hurts a lot?" Hannah said with tears in her eyes.

Mommy took Hannah's hand and held it tight. "Even if it does," she said, "you'll get through it. Would it help if we prayed to God before we went in?"

Hannah nodded and folded her hands together with Mommy. They prayed to God that He would make Hannah strong so that she could get the tests and not have too much pain.

After the tests were over, Hannah and Mommy prayed again–this time to thank God. Hannah said that even when the tests hurt a little, she didn't mind so much because she knew that God was watching over her. Her faith in Him made the tests easier.

Your Turn

1. What made the tests easier for Hannah?

_____

_____

2. How does your faith in God make things easier for you?

_____

_____

Prayer

God, thank You for always helping me. I have faith in You. Amen.

Scary Things

Read this to your child: "Having faith in God makes life easier. If you remember that He is always with you, and you trust Him to help you, even scary things can be easier. Here are some scary things. Can you think of ways in which your faith in God would help you to get through these things? Talk to Mommy or Daddy about it, then finish coloring the pictures."

I Can Get Along with Others

Confrontation

I should confront my problems.

I will be with you and will bless you.

~ Genesis 26:3

Avoiding Daddy

"Why is Caroline still up?" asked Daddy. "Shouldn't she be in bed?"

It was past Caroline's bedtime, but Mommy and Daddy had just seen her sneak around the living room corner. Mommy went to look for Caroline.

"When you find her," said Daddy, "tell her I want to speak to her."

Mommy went to look for Caroline, and soon found her in the bathroom.

"I just had to go potty," she explained, a little scared by the angry look on Mommy's face. "I was already in bed when I had to go."

"That's okay then," said Mommy. "I didn't know you had a good reason for being up. When you're done here, please go see your father."

"Oh, no," said Caroline, afraid her daddy might be angry with her for being out of bed. "I'm going to try to keep him from seeing me!"

Caroline was avoiding her daddy. Avoiding a problem doesn't make it better. In fact, it often makes it worse. A better way to deal with a problem is to simply confront, or face, it.

Caroline was afraid of what her daddy would say to her. But when she confronted her problem and went to see him, she found out all he wanted was to give her a hug and kiss.

You can never hide from your problems, just like you can never hide from God. He will be with you to help you.

Your Turn

1. Why was Caroline afraid to go see Daddy?

_____

_____

2. Why is it impossible to hide from God?

_____

_____

Prayer

Dear God, please help me to remember that it's better to confront my problems. Amen.

What Do You Avoid?

Read this to your child: "Caroline learned that confronting her problem was the best way to overcome it. What do you avoid? Do you think that facing what you're afraid of might make it seem less scary? Here are some things that people sometimes try to avoid. Circle the ones you try to stay away from, and draw an X through the ones that don't bother you. Do you think God wants you to avoid those things you're scared of? Why or why not?"

141

Togetherness

People are more important than things.

A generous man will himself be blessed.

~ Proverbs 22:9

Rachel's Chair

"This is my chair!" yelled Rachel as her cousin Steven leaned against it with his cup of milk. Steven quickly jumped back, sad that Rachel didn't want him there. Still holding his cup of milk, Steven instead sat cross-legged on the floor to drink it.

Rachel started to climb up onto her chair, but then suddenly stopped. She looked up at her cup on the table, and then back down at Steven. She liked having her very own chair to sit in, but all of a sudden, it seemed kind of lonely. She was up high on her special chair, and Steven was way down low on the floor.

Rachel made a decision. Grabbing her cup, she walked over to where Steven sat and snuggled beside him. Neither of them said a word as they quietly sat and drank their milk together.

It can be nice to have some things that are your very own. Rachel had a chair that was hers, but she soon found that being with her cousin was even better than having her own chair.

God teaches that people are more important than things. Being with the people you love is far better than having something to yourself!

Your Turn

1. Why didn't Rachel want Steven to sit on her chair?

_____

_____

2. What do you have that is your very own? Do you share it?

_____

_____

Prayer

God, please help me to remember that being with the people I love is more important than the things I have. Amen.

Homemade Card

Read this to your child: "God teaches that people are more important than things. Rachel forgot that lesson when she yelled at Steven. One way Rachel could have told Steven she was sorry is to make him a special card. You can make one, too. Ask your mommy to fold a piece of paper into fourths. Now draw a picture on the front, and have Mommy write a message for you inside. When you're done, send your card to someone special."

Social Rules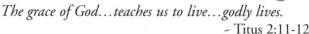

Rules help me know what to do.

The grace of God…teaches us to live…godly lives.

~ Titus 2:11-12

Birdie Toilet

"Mommy!" called Andrea. "The birds went potty in their water!"

Mommy had hung a bird bath on Andrea's pet birds' cage, but the birds had made a mess in the water.

"Mommy," Andrea continued, "maybe you should buy a toilet for them—a little bird toilet."

"Rules are different for animals than they are for people," said Mommy. "There are no toilets for birds like we have for us. We'll just give them some fresh water."

"But baby Ned went to the bathroom in the bathtub water once," remembered Andrea.

"Yes, I know," said Mommy, "but that was wrong."

Rules are different for people than they are for animals. For people, it's not okay to hit, say bad words or spit on the floor. It's also not okay to go to the bathroom in our bath water.

But birds and other animals live a different way. They have different rules that tell them what is and isn't okay to do.

God also gave us rules, called the Ten Commandments. His rules say not to steal or hurt other people, and many more things. God's rules and people rules are important because they help us know what to do.

Your Turn

1. Why is it okay for animals to do things that are not okay for people to do?

_____

_____

2. What does your pet do that you don't?

_____

_____

Prayer

Dear God, thank You for giving us rules that help us live in a way that makes You happy. Amen.

Doing the Right Things

Read this to your child: "In the Bible, God teaches you the right way to do things. There are right and wrong ways to do things in the world around you every day. Match the picture below with the thing that should come next."

Appearances

Things are not always what they seem.

The folly of fools is deception.

~ Proverbs 14:8

Chips or Chips?

Casey loved potato chips. She loved them so much that it didn't matter what flavor they were, ridged or plain, she loved them all.

One day as Casey was helping her mommy work in the flower beds, she noticed that Mommy was picking brown things out of the lawn and putting them back along the edges of the trees.

"What are those things?" Casey asked.

"Those are wood chips," answered Mommy, putting a few more of them around the base of the tree.

"Can we eat those chips?" asked Casey.

"No," said Mommy, "these aren't the kind of chips that you eat. These chips are made of wood."

"Then why are they called chips?" Casey asked.

Mommy explained that sometimes two things can have the same name, but that doesn't mean that they are the same thing.

You shouldn't let yourself be fooled by what something is called. God gave you a brain to make you very smart so that you can figure out what something really is. It's important that you think about things for yourself and not just believe what you see or hear.

Your Turn

1. Why did Casey think that she could eat the wood chips?

_____

_____

2. Can you think of some other things that are called by the same name, but are very different?

_____

_____

Prayer

God, thank You for making me very smart. Amen.

What's What?

Read this to your child: "God made the world and filled it with many wonderful things, but sometimes things aren't what they seem. The flowers below look like flowers, but if you use them a certain way, you'll see that they can also be earrings. Just find some flowers that have joined together in a "V" like the ones in the picture below. Chrysanthemums work especially well for this. If you have a cherry tree nearby (or purchase some cherries at the grocery store), you can find those that grow this way too. To make earrings, simply slide the V over your ear!"

Courtesy

I should treat others as I would like to be treated.

Do to others as you would have them do to you.

~ Luke 6:31

Worm Lesson

One of Rebecca's favorite things to do was gather bugs outside. She could spend hours walking around in the yard, picking up a grasshopper here or a dragonfly there. Grandma and Grandpa had given her a special "bug box" just for her tiny insect friends so she could watch them.

One day Mommy noticed that Rebecca had picked up a worm and thrown it into the flower bed.

"Don't you think you were too rough with that little worm?" asked Mommy with a frown. "You might have hurt it."

"I don't like worms, so I don't care," said Rebecca.

"That's a terrible thing to say," scolded Mommy. "Would you want someone to be mean to you just because he or she didn't like you?"

"Well, no," answered Rebecca quietly as she hung her head low.

"Then you should treat everything and everyone in the same way that you would like to be treated–the way God would want it to be," said Mommy.

It doesn't matter if you like something, or if something is pretty or not, you still need to treat everything the way God teaches. Remember to treat others the way you want to be treated.

Your Turn

1. Why did Rebecca throw the worm into the flower bed?

_____

_____

2. How does God want you to treat others?

_____

_____

Prayer

Dear God, please help me to remember that I should always treat others the way that I would want to be treated. Amen.

Caring About Worms

Read this to your child: "Rebecca learned that God wants us to treat things and people the same way that we would like to be treated, even when we don't like them. In the future, Rebecca was kinder to her bugs. Color Rebecca carefully picking up worms."

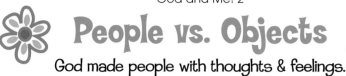

People vs. Objects

God made people with thoughts & feelings.

The Lord knows the thoughts of man.

~ Psalm 94:11

Bad Chair

"Ouch," cried Kyle.

"What happened, Kyle?" cousin Brianna asked as Kyle held his hand over his nose.

"That chair hit me in the nose," Kyle said, wiping the tears from his face as a look of anger replaced his sadness.

"Bad chair," he said, swatting at the chair with his hand. "Bad, bad chair!"

When Brianna saw what Kyle was doing, she began to smile. She was older than her cousin, and she thought what he was doing was silly, but it also looked like fun.

"Naughty, naughty chair," Brianna joined in, as they both began to giggle and run around it.

Kyle and Brianna were treating the chair as if it were a person. Even though Kyle had accidentally bumped into the chair, he blamed the chair for hurting him. Kyle thought that if he scolded it, he wouldn't get hurt by it again.

God made people and objects differently. People have thoughts and feelings, but objects do not. The chair couldn't have hit Kyle because it doesn't have thoughts. Kyle's scolding of the chair wouldn't matter because chairs don't have feelings, either. God only made people with thoughts and feelings.

Your Turn

1. Why did Kyle scold the chair?

_____

_____

2. What did God make with thoughts and feelings?

_____

_____

Prayer

I'm glad You made objects and living creatures in different ways, God. Thank You for giving me thoughts and feelings. Amen.

Living or Thing?

Read this to your child: "People and objects are different. God made people with thoughts and feelings, but objects don't think or feel. In the faces below, draw a person with a bad feeling and a person with a good feeling."

Favoritism

Everyone has different needs.

God does not show favoritism.

~ Romans 2:11

Babying the Baby

Jackie was the new baby in the family, so she got a lot of attention. Not only did Mommy and Daddy give her lots of their time, but her brother and sisters also played with her and cuddled her.

"Why does Jackie get so much attention?" Molly asked Mommy. "It isn't right. I don't like it."

"Jackie gets more attention because she's the baby," explained Mommy. "Jackie needs more of our time because she's so little–just like you did when you were little."

"Everybody needs different things at different times," Mommy continued. "Sometimes your big brother needs help with his homework, and sometimes you need more help doing a puzzle or playing a game. Right now Jackie needs more attention because she's still a baby."

Sometimes other people might get more attention than you do. But it is important to know that God made each of us different with different needs. Also, remember that God is always there for you. He gives everyone the same amount of attention all the time!

Your Turn

1. Are there times you get more attention from Mommy or Daddy than others do?

_____

_____

2. Who will always give you attention?

_____

_____

Prayer

God, please help me to remember that everyone has different needs. Amen.

Equal Chances

Read this to your child: "Sometimes it seems like other people get more attention, but that's because God made each of us with different needs. Here's a game where everyone has an equal chance. Find six paper or plastic cups or containers (they should all be the same size and shape), and place them on the floor as shown. Now borrow 10 pennies from Mommy or Daddy. Standing two feet back from the cups, take turns throwing the pennies into the cups. Whoever gets the most pennies in the farthest cups wins."

Value

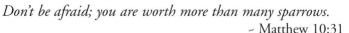

God loves me just because I'm me.

Don't be afraid; you are worth more than many sparrows.
~ Matthew 10:31

Bunny and Bear

Alexandria had a special stuffed bunny that had been a gift from Aunt Leah. She also had a little bear with pink pajamas that Grandma Helen had given her when she was just a baby.

Every night, Alexandria would carefully place the bear and bunny side by side to use as a pillow for her head. She loved the soft, fuzzy feeling of her two favorite "babies" against her cheek as she drifted off to sleep.

One day, Mommy told Alexandria that she was finally old enough to put her crib away and have her very own big girl pillow for her new bed. She no longer would need her bunny and bear each night. The bunny and bear could be put on the shelf with the other toys.

But Alexandria still wanted her special bunny and bear with her in bed at night. Alexandria loved her bunny and bear, even though she wouldn't need them as a pillow anymore. Alexandria has a brand new pillow, but she still cuddled with her special bunny and bear every night as she fell asleep.

Do you love Mommy and Daddy only because they take care of you? Of course not! Loving people isn't about what they can or can't do for you. Love is far too special a feeling for that. In the same way, God loves you not because of what you do or don't do. He loves you just because you're you.

Your Turn

1. Why did Alexandria love her toys?

_____

_____

2. Name some people you love not because of what they do for you but just because you love them.

_____

_____

Prayer

Thank You, God, for loving me just because I'm me. Amen.

Straw Flowers

Read this to your child: "God loves you just for who you are, not for what you do or don't do. Here's a way you can show your love for a special someone: make him or her a special flower! Draw a picture of a flower (only the head, not the stem or leaves) on a piece of paper. Cut out your flower and tape it on the top of a straw. Now you can give your special flower to a special person. You can even make several flowers and stick them in pots inside your house."

Differences

God wants me to care for everyone.

Jesus said, "Take care of my sheep."

~ John 21:16

Peeking at Kylie

"She likes it," said Renee as she and baby Kylie sat on the couch. Renee didn't think Kylie was much fun to play with yet, but Renee and Kylie did have one special game that just the two of them played.

"Where's Kylie?" asked Renee in a squeaky voice. "Peek!" she said as she looked around the hands she had held up to her face. "I see you."

Kylie's eyes were wide with surprise as she smiled at her big sister. She loved this game! As Kylie watched, Renee once again disappeared behind her upheld hands. When Renee peeked out, Kylie again laughed with glee.

Renee loved her sister. She knew Kylie couldn't play yet like older kids because she was too little. So Renee thought of a game that just the two of them could play together. It was her way of doing something that they both could enjoy, and that made them feel closer to each other.

Just like Renee and Kylie, God wants you to find ways to get closer to other people. Even though some people are different from you, God still wants you to try to understand and care for everyone.

Your Turn

1. Why did Renee play the peeking game with Kylie?

_____

_____

2. What do you do when you meet someone who is different from you?

_____

_____

Prayer

God, please help me to remember that even though some people look and act different from me, I can still care for them. Amen.

Getting Along

Read this to your child: "God wants you to care for other people even though they may be different from you. Here are some ways to get to know people. Talk with your mommy or daddy about which ones you have done, and why. Now draw your very own idea in the empty box for getting along with someone."

Attachment

I should be "attached" to Jesus.

It is good to be near God.

~ Psalm 73:28

Blankie and Silkie

Shauna loved her bright yellow blankie. Grandma Opal had bought it for her when she was born.

Shauna took her blankie everywhere, but the day that her family left on vacation, she forgot it. Shauna had been so busy carefully carrying her favorite cup into the van that she forgot her blankie. Her family was a long way from home when Shauna first saw that the blankie was gone. She began to cry.

"Don't worry, Shauna," said Mommy, "I'll buy you a new, special blanket just for our trip."

Daddy stopped the van and they all waited as Mommy went into the store. When she came out, she gave Shauna the most beautiful pink blanket with satin trim that Shauna had ever seen. It was so soft that Shauna named it "Silkie." She still missed her yellow blankie very much, but Silkie kept her feeling warm and safe until she got back home.

After the vacation was over, Shauna was never seen without blankie and Silkie by her side. Now she had two special blankets!

Shauna was very attached to her blankets. That means that she loved them and wanted to be near them all the time. You should feel that way about God, too. You should not only love Him, but want to be near Him. You can be near to God by praying, doing what the Bible teaches and thinking about Him every day.

Your Turn

1. How did Shauna's blankie and Silkie make her feel? Do you have a blankie?

_____

_____

2. How can you be near to God every day?

_____

_____

Prayer

Thank You, God, for being so "attached" to me! Amen.

Puppet Girl

Read this to your child: "You should always want to be near to God by learning about Him, listening to the Bible and trying to do what He teaches. Here's something you can make that will be near to you. Draw a face on the bottom of a lunch sack. Have your mommy or daddy cut holes where the arms would be. Slide the bag onto your hand, and put a finger through each hole. Now you have a puppet girl!"

Sacrifice

Jesus sacrificed His life for me.

He is the…sacrifice for our sins.

~ 1 John 2:2

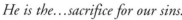

Messy Miranda

Miranda didn't like it when Mommy had to go to work, but she loved having Grandma babysit her. Grandma would read stories, snuggle on the couch and sing songs.

Grandma would also let Miranda do things that Mommy didn't, such as feed herself. Mommy didn't like Miranda to feed herself because she said it was too messy, but Miranda thought it was fun.

One day when Mommy was away at work, Grandma put Miranda in the high chair and gave her a bowl of strained pears. *Yum, yum,* thought Miranda as she reached into the bowl, but Grandma stopped her.

"Use the spoon, honey," said Grandma as she put a spoon in her hand.

Slowly and carefully, Miranda used the spoon to scoop up some of the runny pears, but they never made it to her mouth. Miranda was soon covered with pears! But after some practice, she could bring the pears to her mouth. She had made a big mess, but she had learned something important. She could feed herself like a big girl!

Sometimes we have to sacrifice one thing to get another. Miranda's grandma knew that she would have to sacrifice cleaning up a mess for Miranda to learn to feed herself. And it was well worth it!

Jesus sacrificed His life to save us from our sins. That was the most important sacrifice that has ever happened

Your Turn

1. Why didn't Miranda's mommy want her to feed herself?

_____

_____

2. Tell about a time you sacrificed something in order to get something else.

_____

_____

Prayer

Thank You, Jesus, for sacrificing Your life for me. Amen.

Paper Crown

Read this to your child: "Jesus sacrificed His life to save you from your sins. Sometimes you must also sacrifice one thing to get another. Here's an activity where all you have to sacrifice is a little time and a paper bag. Just cut off the open end of a paper bag (as shown). Cut a triangle pattern on the other end. Now you have a paper crown! Color your crown and pretend you are a princess."

Friendship

Even though I can't see Him, God is my friend.

A friend loves at all times.

~ Proverbs 17:17

Long-distance Friends

"Can Jacob and I be friends?" Kaylee asked Mommy. "Can he come over and play computer games with me sometime?"

Kaylee had just spent the evening playing with some of her parents' friends' kids. They lived far away, so this was the first time she'd met them.

"Jacob lives too far away for that," answered Mommy. "That's why we write letters and call each other instead of visiting very often."

"Well, can't we still be friends?" asked Kaylee again. "You're friends with his parents and you don't visit often, so why can't I be friends with Jacob, too?"

As Mommy thought about that, Kaylee continued, "Jacob and I both like computer games a lot, we're close to the same age and we had lots and lots of fun together. We'd be good friends."

"I guess you're right," said Mommy. "The two of you could write or e-mail each other. You could be pen pals! How does that sound?"

Kaylee thought that sounded great!

People don't have to live near each other, or see each other all the time, to be friends. Friendship is about sharing and caring in good times and bad.

In the same way, even though you don't see God by your side every day, you know He's there. He's a good friend. You can feel His love and guidance every day.

Your Turn

1. Why did Mommy say they couldn't visit Jacob?

_____

_____

2. Do you have any friends who live far away?

_____

_____

Prayer

Dear God, please help me to remember that I can be friends with people who live far away and care about them, as You care about me. Amen.

Staying Friends

Read this to your child: "Even though you can't see God, He's always beside you, taking good care of you. In the same way, even though you may not be able to get together with a friend very often, he or she can still be your friend. Here are some ways you can stay close to friends who live far away. Have you ever used any of these ways to keep in touch with friends? Can you think of any more ways?"

Cooperation

I should cooperate.

Live in harmony with one another.

~ 1 Peter 3:8

Christina's Alphabet

Christina didn't like learning the alphabet. When Mommy practiced with her, Christina would act like she didn't understand. Today was no different.

"Christina," Mommy said, holding up a letter card, "what letter is this?"

Christina looked at the letter "A" and simply said, "Bird."

"What about the alphabet song?" Mommy asked, starting to sing.

Christina just looked at Mommy, and said, "Rock."

Mommy didn't know what to do. Christina just wouldn't cooperate! Every day, Christina said any word that came into her head instead of reading the letters off of the cards that Mommy showed her. And every day, Mommy got sadder and sadder because she didn't know what to do to help Christina learn.

One day as Mommy was working in the flower garden, Christina didn't know that Mommy could hear her through the open window. To Mommy's surprise, she heard Christina singing the alphabet song perfectly. She really did know her alphabet all along!

Christina did a bad thing. She didn't like that she had to practice, so she wouldn't cooperate with Mommy when she was teaching her. She let her mommy think that she wasn't able to learn, and that made her mommy sad.

God wants you to cooperate with your parents, and learn as much as you can. Only when you cooperate can you be at your best, as God plans for you.

Your Turn

1. How did Christina make her mommy sad?

_____

_____

2. How do you cooperate?

_____

_____

Prayer

God, please help me to remember that I should cooperate with others so I can be my best for You. Amen.

Alphabet Animals

Read this to your child: "Christina didn't cooperate with her mommy, which made her mommy sad. God wants you to cooperate with your parents because He gave you to them so they could help you be your best. Here are some of the letters that Christina acted like she didn't know. Do you know them? Draw a line from each letter to the animal whose name begins with that letter."

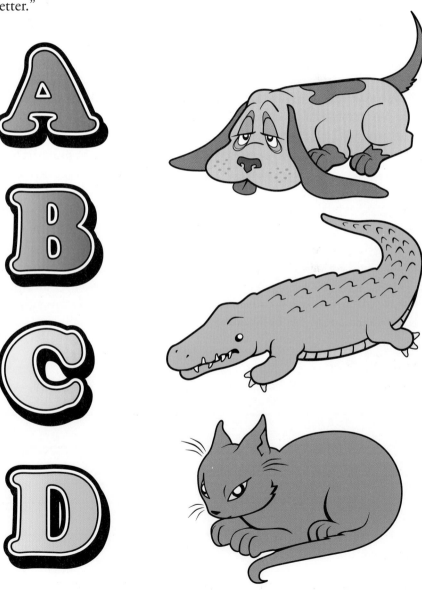

Trust

I can trust that God is always with me.

Trust in him at all times.

~ Psalm 62:8

Madison's Trust

Madison's family was vacationing in Michigan, seeing wonderful sights such as giant trees and huge sand dunes, and swimming in the big lakes. It was a lot of fun, but Madison couldn't wait to see the waterfalls.

As Madison and her daddy walked the long trail to the waterfall, she could hear the sound of the water pouring over the falls. The sound got louder and louder as she grew closer.

When Madison finally got to the end of the trail, she couldn't believe her eyes. The waterfall was so big and so loud!

As she walked along the edge of the viewing platform, Daddy followed. Madison didn't see Daddy because she was looking at the waterfall, but she knew that he was there. Once, when Madison stepped a little too close to the edge, Daddy's hand lightly touched her shoulder and pulled her back.

The waterfall was kind of scary even though it was beautiful, but Madison was never worried, because she knew Daddy would never let her get hurt. Madison trusted her daddy so much that she never even had to look at him to know that he was still there. She knew that he would take care of her.

In the same way, you can trust God to watch over you, even though you can't see Him. Just like Madison's daddy, God is always by your side, guiding your steps and ready to pull you back if you move too closely toward danger.

Your Turn

1. Why didn't Madison have to worry about getting too close to the waterfall?

_____

_____

2. Besides Mommy and Daddy, whom can you trust to watch over you?

_____

_____

Prayer

Thank You, God, for always being near me. I trust You. Amen.

Cork Snake

Read this to your child: "You should always trust God, because even though you can't see Him, He is always by your side. Here's an activity that you'll need to trust your mommy or daddy for help. Have Mommy or Daddy connect several corks (from bottles or a craft store) with a needle and thread, leaving a little space between each. Use a pencil to make eyes on the first cork. Glue on a small, red tongue made from felt. Your "snake" will float in the bathtub, and because the corks aren't tied together too tightly, it will really appear to swim like a snake!"

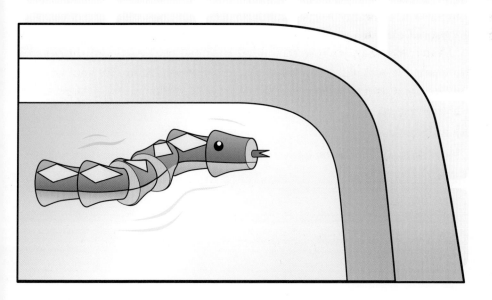

Communication
God knows how I feel.

God knows your hearts.

~ Luke 16:15

Tummy With a Sore Throat

Mariah didn't feel good. She rubbed her stomach with her hand.
"What's wrong, honey?" Mommy asked. "Are you all right?"
"I don't know," answered Mariah.
"Does your head hurt?" asked Mommy.
"No," said Mariah, as Mommy put her hand on Mariah's forehead.
"You don't feel like you have a fever," said Mommy. "Is your throat sore?"
"No," said Mariah again. "My throat's not sore."
"Then what, sweetheart? Can you tell me what's wrong?" Mommy asked.
"No," said Mariah.
"I know," said Mommy suddenly. "It's your stomach, isn't it?"
Mariah looked surprised. How did Mommy know? Mariah nodded and said, "My tummy has a sore throat."
Without being told, Mommy knew that Mariah didn't feel good. Even though Mariah was not able to tell Mommy what was wrong, Mommy could figure it out. Mommy knew Mariah so well that they didn't need words to understand each other.
God is like that. It's nice to sing to Him and pray every day, but even if you don't, He will still know what you're thinking. He knows you and how you feel, no matter what you say.

Your Turn

1. How does your mommy know how you feel, even when you don't tell her?

_____

_____

2. Who always knows what you're thinking and how you feel?

_____

_____

Prayer

God, thank You for knowing me so well that I don't need words to make You understand me. Amen.

Communicating with God

Read this to your child: "You don't need words to make God understand how you're feeling or what you're thinking. He always knows. Even though you don't need words to make God understand you, it's nice to tell Him sometimes. Here are some ways to show God how you feel. Discuss each of them with your mommy or daddy. Do you do any of these?"

Consideration

I should be considerate of others.

Clothe yourselves with compassion.

~ Colossians 3:12

Sore Knees

Isabel and her little sister, Laura, sat in the doctor's examining room, waiting for him to come in. Isabel had hurt her knee, and she needed the doctor to take a look at it.

When the doctor came into the room, Isabel was surprised to see her little sister pull up her pant leg and start talking to the doctor.

"I have a boo-boo on my leg," said Laura as she pointed to her knee.

Mommy started to tell the doctor that Laura wasn't there to be looked at, but he bent down to look at Laura's knee anyway.

"Oh, I see," said the doctor "but it looks okay. It will be better soon."

As the doctor turned his attention toward Isabel, Laura smiled. Even though the doctor wasn't there to see her, and he was very busy, he took the time to listen to her. The doctor was considerate of Laura.

God wants you to be considerate of others as the doctor was. No matter how busy you are, or what else you need to do, you should listen to other people and treat them nicely. Treating people with consideration makes God happy.

Your Turn

1. Why did Laura want the doctor to look at her knee?

_____

_____

2. Do you always treat people with consideration? How do you do that?

_____

_____

Prayer

God, please help me to remember that no matter how busy I am, I should treat people with consideration. Amen.

Cardboard Top

Read this to your child: "No matter how busy you are, or how much you have to do, God still wants you to be considerate of others. You should always take the time to listen and be nice to others. Here's a fun project that Isabel and Laura like to make together. Because they are considerate of each other, they love working together to make these fun tops. Find some cardboard, and draw a circle on it (you can use a water glass or soup can to outline the circle). Now color the circle and cut it out. Push a stick, pencil (or a pin, if Mommy or Daddy are doing it) through the center. Now spin your top!"

Helpfulness

I should do what's best for other people.

Love your neighbor as yourself.

~ Leviticus 19:18

Jade's Quarter

Jade saw the shiny quarter half-hidden among the wood chips on the ground. As the other kids played on the slides and swings, Jade picked up the quarter and ran to her mommy.

"Look what I found," said Jade.

"Let's ask if anyone lost some money," said Mommy, looking around at the other children.

"No!" said Jade. "It's mine. I found it."

"But how would you feel if you lost a quarter and somebody found it but didn't give it back to you?" said Mommy. "Don't you think you'd feel bad? Wouldn't you want the other person to give the quarter back to you?"

Jade thought about what Mommy said. She knew that she would feel bad if she lost her quarter, and she would want it back. Jade decided to find the person who lost the quarter. When she couldn't, she decided to put it in the church offering plate the next Sunday.

Jade did the right thing. God loves you and does what's best for you, so you should love other people and try to help them whenever you can as well. Jade tried to find the owner of the quarter, but when she couldn't, she gave the quarter to the church so the money would go to helping others.

Your Turn

1. Why did Jade want to keep the quarter?

_____

_____

2. Have you ever found something that belonged to someone else? What did you do?

_____

_____

Prayer

God, please help me to remember that it's important to help others whenever I can. Amen.

Coin Shaker

Read this to your child: "God wants you to love and help other people whenever you can, just as He loves and helps you. Here's something you can do with quarters, or any other coins you have around the house. Have Mommy or Daddy save an empty paper towel tube for you. Use tape (or a rubber band) to secure a piece of cardboard over one end. Now place several coins (a mixture of sizes is best) into the tube, and cover the other end. Shake the tube. What does it sound like? Can you make a rhythm?"

Note to parents: Don't put too many coins (especially quarters) into the tube, or they may break through the ends.

Flattery

Flattery should only be used to make others happy.

Do to others what you would have them do to you.

~ Matthew 7:12

You're Pretty

"Mom, you're very pretty," said Kiara as her mommy got into the car. She wanted some candy, and she thought that if she could make Mommy smile, she'd have a better chance of getting some.

"Oh, thank you, honey," said Mommy. "That's so nice."

"You're pretty," said Kiara again, putting on her best smile. Mommy paused and smiled in return as she stroked her fingers through Kiara's hair, and then checked that her car seat belt was on tight. She knew that Kiara wanted some candy, but she also felt very warm and good inside hearing her say such nice things to her.

"What a nice girl you are," Mommy said, smiling again. "You've been such a good girl, would you like a lollipop?"

Flattery is a good thing, when it is done for a good reason. God wants you to make people happy whenever you can. Just be sure you do it for good reasons. God only wants you to be nice if you really mean it, not just to get something for yourself.

Your Turn

1. Why did Kiara tell her mommy she was pretty?

_____

_____

2. Have you ever used flattery to get what you want?

_____

_____

Prayer

God, please help me to remember that I should only use flattery to make others feel happy. Amen.

Fancy Lollipop

Read this to your child: "God wants you to use flattery only to make others feel happy, not just to get something you want. Here's a picture of Kiara's lollipop for you to color. It's very fancy, so you can use many different colors."

Attention

I will always get love and attention from God.

The Lord Almighty will care for his flock.
~ Zechariah 10:3

Always a Baby

"I can't believe how big you're getting," said Mommy as she slipped a dress over Hilary's head. "You're growing up too fast."

Hilary scowled as she said, "I'm not growing up big!"

"You're going to stay small?" Mommy asked, surprised.

"Yes," Hilary answered simply.

"Oh," said Mommy, suddenly understanding. "You're always going to be my baby?"

"Yes," answered Hilary as she started to giggle.

"Okay," said Mommy. "You can always be my baby–even if you grow up big, you can still be my baby. No matter how big you get, I'll still snuggle you like my baby, give you baby kisses and help you get dressed."

Hilary liked that.

Mommy figured out that Hilary wanted to stay a baby because then she would get extra attention from Mommy. Hilary didn't know that children are always precious babies in their parents' eyes, no matter how big they get to be.

In the same way, no matter how big you get, or how you change, you are always God's child, too. You will always get just as much love and attention from God, no matter how old you get to be.

Your Turn

1. What did Mommy say she'd keep doing for "baby" Hilary?

_____

_____

2. Would you like to stay a baby? Why or why not?

_____

_____

Prayer

God, thank You for giving me just as much love and attention no matter how big I get, or how old I am. Amen.

Special Attention

Read this to your child: "God will always give you just as much love and attention, no matter how old you are. Below are some ways that mommies and daddies give their babies special attention. Circle the ones that your mommy or daddy does for you."

Care

I should take care of others.

As I have loved you, so you must love one another.

~ John 13:34

Taking Care of Others

Fallon wanted another parakeet. She already had one, but she knew that in order for her bird to have babies, she would need two birds.

"Please, Mommy," Fallon begged, "please get me another bird so that they can lay eggs. I want babies so much."

"I don't know," said Mommy, "one bird is already a lot of work for you. Two would be even more work. You would have to fill the seed and water cups every day, and change the paper. I just don't know if you can do it."

"Yes, I can," said Fallon. "I can take care of both birds. I know I can! Just give me a chance."

It was two whole days before Mommy finally decided that Fallon could have another bird. From the day that the new bird came home, Fallon took extra good care of it. She knew that the birds needed her to keep them clean and fed, and she was a good pet owner.

Fallon took good care of her pets. She made sure that they had everything they needed because it was her job. In the same way, God wants you to feel it is your job to take care of others. You should do everything you can to take care of people whenever you can, just as God takes care of you.

Your Turn

1. Why did Fallon want another bird?

_____

_____

2. Do you take good care of others? Why, or why not?

_____

_____

Prayer

God, please help me to know how to care for others best, and to do as much as I can. Amen.

Counting "Keets"

Read this to your child: "God wants you to take care of others as much as you can. Here are some pictures of Fallon's parakeets. They form letters. Can you guess which ones? Can you count how many blue, orange and yellow parakeets are in each letter?"

Charity

Charity is good, no matter how I do it.

Whoever sows generously will also reap generously.

~ 2 Corinthians 9:6

Pies for People

Kelly sprinkled flour into the pie pan, giggling at how the white powder stuck to her fingers.

"Remember to do all the pans," said Mommy. "We don't want to miss any. We said we'd bring several pies."

"Okay, Mommy," Kelly answered. She was proud to be helping Mommy make the pies for church. Mommy said that they were helping people who lived far, far away by making the pies, but she wondered how that could be.

"Mommy," Kelly asked, "how is making pies going to help those people? How can the mailman get the pies there?"

"The mailman won't take the pies there," explained Mommy. "We'll take the pies to church, and then they'll sell them. Then the church will send the money to a place that buys things those people need. That's how our church's charity works."

Charity isn't always about doing or giving something directly. Sometimes it's about helping someone to help others. Either way, charity is a good thing. God wants you to help other people, no matter which way you do it.

Your Turn

1. Why were Kelly and Mommy making pies?

_____

_____

2. What do you do to help other people?

_____

_____

Prayer

God, please help me to remember that it's a good thing to help other people, no matter how I do it. Amen.

Making Pies

Read this to your child: "God wants you to help other people, even if it's by helping someone else to help others. Here's a picture of Kelly helping her Mommy bake pies for church for you to color (turn the book sideways to see it correctly). Finish coloring the picture."

I Can Learn About God's World

The Sun

God made the sun to keep us warm and help things grow.

God said, "Let there be light," and there was light.

~ Genesis 1:3

Bothersome Sun

"Mommy, the sun is bothering me," said Jenna. She was trying to watch TV, but the morning sun was bright and hot through the window. It was shining in her eyes as she looked at the TV screen.

"Well, you just tell that ol' sun to stop bothering you," Mommy said with a smile.

"I can't," said Jenna. "The sun doesn't have a mouth."

"It doesn't need a mouth to hear you tell it to leave you alone. It just needs ears to hear you," Mommy laughed.

"The sun doesn't have ears either," said Jenna very seriously. "It can't hear me, and I want it gone."

"You shouldn't say that," answered Mommy. "The sun is very important. If God hadn't made the sun, we would be very cold, and nothing on earth could live."

Sometimes even very important, good things can bother you, but that doesn't mean that you should wish them away. God made the sun hot and bright to keep you warm and help plants grow. You should be thankful.

Your Turn

1. Why did God make the sun?

_____

_____

2. What do you like most about the sun?

_____

_____

Prayer

Thank You, God, for making the sun hot and bright so that I can stay warm, and plants can grow. Amen.

Shapes and Colors

Read this to your child: "God made everything in the world. Each thing has its own shape and color. Look at all the wonderful things that God made below. Can you name each one? Now color them."

Darkness

I don't need to be afraid of the dark, because God takes care of me.

The darkness he called "night."

~ Genesis 1:5

Lighting the Way

"I want to take it to bed with me," said Kelsey as she pointed to Daddy's big, black flashlight.

"I don't think that's a good idea," said Mommy. "You don't need a flashlight in bed with you anyway."

"Yes, I do," cried Kelsey. "It's dark in my room, and the flashlight will keep me safe."

"How will the light keep you safe?" Mommy asked.

"It will make it less dark so I don't have to be scared," Kelsey answered.

"You don't have to be scared whether it's dark or light," Mommy said. "God will always take care of you, whether the lights are on or off. You don't need to be afraid of the dark."

You don't have to be afraid of the dark, either. Darkness is a natural part of the world that God created. God is with you, taking care of you, whether it's dark or light, so you never need to be afraid. He lights your way better than any flashlight ever could!

Your Turn

1. Why shouldn't Kelsey be afraid of the dark?

_____

_____

2. Are you ever afraid of the dark? Why, or why not?

_____

_____

Prayer

Dear God, please help me to remember that You are always with me, even in the dark. Amen.

Homemade Light

Read this to your child: "God is always with you, even in the dark. You can make your own special flashlight for playing in the dark. Cut a fun shape in the end of an empty oatmeal container. In the other end, cut a hole just big enough to insert a flashlight. Now you have a special flashlight to shine shapes on a dark wall! (Turn the book sideways to see it correctly.)"

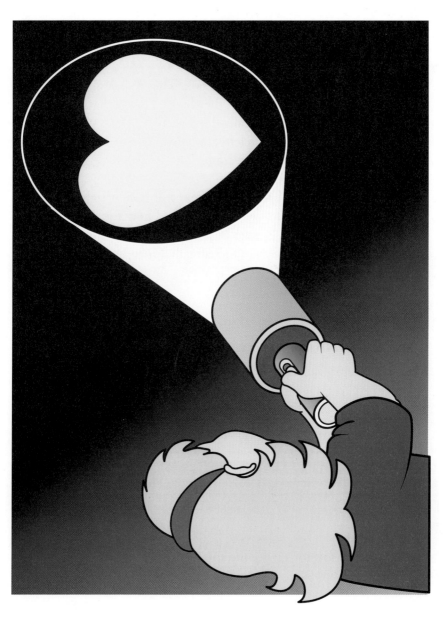

Time

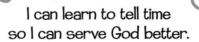

I can learn to tell time so I can serve God better.

There is a time for everything.

~ Ecclesiastes 3:1

Telling Time by Letters

"What time is it?" asked Mommy.

"There's an upside-down L and a backward E," answered Riley.

"There aren't any letters on the clock," said Mommy. "A clock has numbers on it. That is how you tell time."

"But there are letters," said Riley. "Look. They're just all messed up!"

When Mommy looked closely at the clock, she saw that Riley was telling the truth. Some of the numbers really did look like letters! When Riley finally understood that what looked like letters were really numbers, she soon found that she could learn how to tell the time.

"Is it 7:15?" asked Riley.

"Yes," said Mommy. "That's better. Now you have it right!"

Riley was very happy. She finally understood how to tell time.

It is important to know how to tell time. Ask your mommy or daddy to help you learn to tell time if you don't already know how. That way you can use your time well and serve God. It is always time to live for God!

Your Turn

1. Why is learning to tell time important?

_____

_____

2. How can you serve God by knowing how to tell time?

_____

_____

Prayer

Dear God, thank You for giving me the gift of time. Please help me to learn how to use it well. Amen.

Numbers or Letters?

Read this to your child: "Learning how to tell time is important for many reasons, but especially so you can serve God better. In our story, Riley thought the clock numbers looked like letters. Take a look at the numbers below. Can you fix them so they look the right way? Now draw the clock hands until the clock says 7:15 as Riley's clock did."

Fire

God does not want me to play with matches.

The one who started the fire must make restitution.

~ Exodus 22:6

Fire Burns

"I'm going to make a fire in my room," said Leslie as she held a matchbook in her hand.

"Please give those matches to your mommy," said Aunt Donna. Leslie's mommy had just used the matches to light a birthday cake. She had taken them when her mommy wasn't looking.

"No," answered Leslie. "I'm going to take these into my room and make a camp fire."

"Leslie," said Aunt Donna, "matches are very dangerous. The fire that they make doesn't just burn wood in campfires. Fire can burn whole houses and people."

Leslie thought about what Aunt Donna said. She still thought that making a fire in her room would be a lot of fun, but she also didn't want anyone to get hurt. Leslie gave the matches to her mommy.

Many of the things God gives you, such as fire, can be used for good. But they also can be used in the wrong way. Fire is good, but it can be dangerous. God wants you to use what He gives you for the right reasons. That is why you should never play with matches. Only adults should make fires.

Your Turn

1. How is playing with matches a bad thing?

_____

_____

2. Why does God not want you to play with matches?

_____

_____

Prayer

Dear God, thank You for giving me fire. Please help me to remember that fire can be dangerous, and I should never play with matches. Amen.

Bubble Straw

Read this to your child: "Playing with matches is very dangerous. God wants you to use what He gives you for the right reasons. He wants you to be safe and healthy. Here's something to play with that's much more fun than matches, and a lot safer, too. Just pour a small amount of dish soap into a small dish of water. Dip one end of a straw into the water mixture. Now blow into the dry end of the straw. Watch the bubbles form and float up into the air!"

Music

God wants me to praise Him with music.

I will make music to the Lord.

~ Judges 5:3

Wrong Words, Right Sound

"He's singing the wrong words," said Jillian. "Stop him. Tell him to do it right!"

Jillian loved music, but she didn't like it when her little brother, Ethan, sang the wrong words. As Jillian frowned, baby Ethan sang, "Bitsy bitsy 'pider, up a water pout!" as loud as he could.

"Stop him!" Jillian cried again.

Ethan heard Jillian, but he thought it was funny to tease her so he sang another song: "Jesus loves me oh, oh, oh."

"He's still doing it!" Jillian cried as she covered her ears with her hands as tightly as she could. "I can't stand it!"

Jillian didn't understand that it's not the words that matter as much as the meaning behind them. Whether or not Ethan had the right words didn't matter as much as that Ethan loved to make music.

Can you sing, play an instrument or tap a rhythm? God loves when you make music, especially when you are praising Him.

Your Turn

1. Does it matter that Ethan wasn't singing all of the right words?

_____

_____

2. What is a praise song you like to sing to God?

_____

_____

Prayer

Thank You, God, for liking my songs, even if I don't get all the words right. And thank You for loving me, too. Amen.

Whistle Time

Read this to your child: "God loves when you praise Him with music. Here is a fun whistle you can make to play and praise God. Cut a piece of paper into a strip 6 inches long by 1½ inches wide. Fold the paper strip in half. With the fold facing down, cut an upside-down V into the folded side (the dimensions don't have to be specific, but for ours the edges of the V come in about ¼ inch from each side, and the tip of the V is about ¾ inches high). Pinch the paper between the first two fingers of one hand, with your fingers parallel to the folded edge and resting just above the tip of the V. Now fold each side of the unfolded edge of the paper back, one side over each finger. Press the paper lightly to your lips and part your fingers slightly. Blow down through the center of the paper and into the V. It helps if you purse your lips slightly, and give hard blows!"

Animals

God gave us animals to love and use.

God made the wild animals according to their kinds.
~ Genesis 1:25

Factory Chicken

What a wonderful summer, thought Annabel. Daddy had brought home a whole box full of baby chickens. Annabel knew what they were before he even opened the box because they were peeping so loudly.

When Daddy opened the box, Annabel knew it was one of the most wonderful sights she had ever seen. The chicks were yellow and fuzzy! Annabel loved to hold the chicks close to her and feel their feathers against her skin.

As the baby chicks grew, Daddy built them a coop. Even though they lived outside and grew into big chickens, Annabel still loved them. She even had names for them!

One day as Mommy was roasting a chicken for dinner, Annabel asked, "Is that a real chicken or a factory chicken?"

Mommy thought for a minute. "Well," she answered, "the chicken I'm cooking came from the grocery store, but it's a real chicken."

Seeing Annabel's worried face Mommy quickly added, "But it's not one of our chickens."

Annabel was happy to know her Mommy wasn't cooking one of her pet chickens. However, God did give us animals to love and use. Even though we sometimes have animals as pets, it is in God's plan for us to use other animals for food, too.

Your Turn

1. Why did Annabel want to know which chicken Mommy was cooking?

_____

_____

2. Who made the animals for us to love and use?

_____

_____

Prayer

Thank You, God, for giving us animals to love and use. Amen.

Real Animals

Read this to your child: "God gave us animals to love and use. Annabel had baby chicks that grew up to be chickens. Animals start out as babies and then grow larger. Draw a line from the baby animal below to what it looks like when it grows up."

Nature

God's world is a miracle.

His invisible nature…has been clearly perceived
in the things that have been made.

~ Romans 1:20

Amazing Eggs

The chicken sat in its nest box, softly clucking as it laid another pearly white egg. Veronica stood with her basket in her hand, eager to gather the eggs and take them into the house. She loved to be the first person to touch the eggs.

Veronica waited and waited, but today the chicken didn't get off the nest box. It just kept sitting there. Veronica wondered if the chicken would peck her if she reached under to get the eggs. Would it squawk? Would it fly into Veronica's face? Maybe it would even jump up and break the eggs by standing on them!

Veronica didn't know what would happen, but she couldn't wait any longer. She slowly walked up to the chicken and carefully reached underneath. The feathers were silky soft on Veronica's hand as she reached into the warmth below. The chicken raised itself up a little for Veronica to get the eggs, as if it wanted them to be taken out.

Veronica took an egg and stepped back. It was warm! Veronica felt excited just thinking about what a wondrous thing it was to hold a just-laid egg in her hand.

The world is such a wonderful, amazing place! Even the smallest thing, like an egg, is like a miracle. God's world is a miracle.

Your Turn

1. What's so special about an egg?

_____

_____

2. Can you name some things in God's creation that you think are miracles?

_____

_____

Prayer

Thank You, God, for all the miracles in our world. Amen.

What Jesus Made

Read this to your child: "God made everything in nature. He made trees, flowers and all the animals. The pictures below show what God made and what you can make. Circle what God made and draw a square around what you can make with His help."

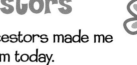

Ancestors

God and my ancestors made me who I am today.

I am no better than my ancestors.

~ 1 Kings 19:4

Sophie's Ancestors

Sophie was learning about ancestors in kindergarten. She learned that ancestors are people who were part of her family long before she was born, and who weren't alive anymore. They had babies, and their babies grew up to have babies, and so on, until the day that Sophie was finally born.

"What did my ancestors do?" Sophie asked Mommy one day. "Did they fight in the Civil War?"

"No," answered Mommy, "our ancestors weren't in this country then."

Sophie thought about what Mommy had said, but it didn't make sense to her. "Did our ancestors hide in the woods 'til the battle was over, and then come out and have babies?" she asked.

"No," answered Mommy. "Our ancestors were still in Germany then. They came to this country much later."

Sophie was learning about her ancestors—the people in her family who came before her. Without your ancestors, you wouldn't be alive today. Who they were and what they did helped to make you who you are.

In the same way, who God is (and what He did for you) has made you who you are today. Without Him, you wouldn't be saved from your sins, and you wouldn't have the Bible and all His teachings to show you how to live.

Your Turn

1. What are "ancestors"?

_____

_____

2. How does God make you who you are?

_____

_____

Prayer

Thank You, God, for coming before me, saving me from my sins and teaching me how to live. Amen.

Music Makers

Read this to your child: "God made the very first people, named Adam and Eve. They had babies, and their babies grew up to have babies, and so on until you came along. Your ancestors did many things different from you. One thing that has changed a lot is how we make music. Your ancestors might have made music by rubbing or banging two different things together to make a funny sound. They had to use whatever they had around them in those days. To try it, ask your mommy for two pie tins or some pots and pans. Clang the tins together like cymbals, or bang on the pots and pans with a spoon like a drum. It's fun!"

Magic

There is no such thing as magic.

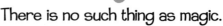

I am against your magic.

~ Ezekiel 13:20

Ding-a-Ding-Ding

Deirdra loved to go shopping with Grandma. They always looked at toys and games. Sometimes they even went to the pet store.

Grandma played CDs in the car on their way to the store. Every time they came to a stop light, she would say "ding-a-ding-ding" just before the light changed from red to green. She said it was "magic" and that she knew how to make the light change color.

Deirdra had believed Grandma, but today was different. She had been watching when she was in the car with Mommy, and she noticed that the light still changed color even though Mommy never said, "Ding-a-ding-ding."

As Grandma pulled to a stop before the stoplight, she said to Deirdra, "Now watch. The light is going to change…ding-a-ding-ding!"

Grandma was surprised that Deirdra didn't laugh when the light changed. This time, Deirdra looked at Grandma with a serious face and said, "Grandma, that doesn't work." Grandma laughed and admitted she had been playing a game with Deirdra. She really wasn't causing the light to change!

Sometimes what seems like magic is just something you don't understand. Once you know how and why things work, then you know they are not magic anymore. God wants you to trust in Him and not put your faith in magic. There is no such thing as magic. Everything comes from God!

Your Turn

1. Did Grandma really know magic?

_____

_____

2. Is it better to put your faith in magic or in God? Why?

_____

_____

Prayer

Dear God, please help me to remember that there is no such thing as magic, but that everything comes from You. Amen.

Jar Garden

Read this to your child: "Many things can seem like magic if you don't know how they work. But really, everything has a reason–and everything comes from God. A Jar Garden is something that can seem like magic. Do plants need water? Of course they do! But did you know that if you plant some seeds inside of a glass jar, you'll never need to water them? They water themselves! To see this in action, wash out the largest glass jar you can find. Lay the jar on its side and spread a shallow layer of small stones or gravel in it. Then smooth a deep layer of potting soil over the gravel. Now add the plants. You can use seeds, but it is easier to start with a few small plants (such as ivy or ferns). Sprinkle a small amount of water over your plants, and put the lid on your jar. Now place your jar in a warm, sunny spot and watch your plants grow!"

Consequences

Every choice I make has a cost.

Sit down and estimate the cost.

~ Luke 14:28

The Cost of Amy's Choice

Amy had a favorite pink blanket that she slept with each night. She loved how soft and fuzzy it was, and she also liked the silky edging it had around it.

Each night, she would pull and tug at the silk until a section of it came loose from the blanket. Then Amy would put her head through the hole. It was a dangerous thing to do because Amy was very little and could easily choke herself with the silky edging.

Every day Amy's mommy would carefully sew the silk back to the pink blanket, and each night Amy would once again tear it loose. This went on for several days until Mommy finally came to a decision. Mommy decided that it was just too dangerous to leave the silk on the blanket, so she pulled out all of the stitches, and completely removed the silk from Amy's blanket.

There are consequences for everything we choose to do. Amy chose to keep tearing the silk off of her blanket. Her choice to do that caused her to lose her silky border completely.

In the same way, if you choose not to believe in God, and don't do what He tells you, then you can't be with Him in heaven someday. God wants you to be careful about the choices you make, because everything has consequences.

Your Turn

1. Why did Amy's mommy take the silk off of her blanket?

_____

_____

2. Why is it important to make choices carefully?

_____

_____

Prayer

Dear God, please help me to make my choices carefully, remembering that everything has consequences. Amen.

Carrot Top

Read this to your child: "God wants you to make your choices carefully because everything has consequences. In this activity, if you choose to let the water dry up, the carrot top will stop growing. To do the activity, cut the top off of a carrot. Place the top in a small saucer of water so that just the base of the carrot top is in the water. Set the saucer in a warm, sunny place and check each day to make sure that the water doesn't dry up. After a couple of weeks, what do you see? Your carrot will be growing a new green top!"

Monsters

There is no such thing as monsters.

The Lord is with us. Do not be afraid.

~ Numbers 14:9

Monsters?

"Will you protect me from monsters?" asked Savannah.

"Yes, Savannah," answered Mommy, "I'll protect you from the monsters."

"Will monsters eat me?" asked Savannah.

"No, sweetie," said Mommy, "the monsters won't eat you. I'll protect you."

Savannah thought there were monsters in the world. She believed that creatures would hide in her closet at night or chase her after dark–but that's not true.

When you're little, there's a lot you don't know yet, and that's why it can be easy to believe in monsters. As you get older and learn more about the world and the way things work, you'll see that there are no "monsters" because that's not the way God made the world.

Scary things sometimes happen, and people sometimes do bad things, but that doesn't mean there are actual "monsters." If you are scared, ask your mommy or daddy to pray with you. God will protect you.

Your Turn

1. Is there any such thing as monsters? Why or why not?

_____

_____

2. What can you do when you're scared?

_____

_____

Prayer

Thank You, Jesus, for making a world that doesn't have monsters in it. Amen.

Toothpick Porcupine

Read this to your child: "God didn't make monsters, so you don't need to be afraid of them. They don't exist! Here's a creature you can make that's silly, not scary. Set a lemon on its side. Stick four toothpicks into it for legs. On the opposite side, stick many toothpicks all over it, except for the end of the lemon that is slightly tapered (leave that bare). The pointy end looks like a nose. Draw eyes above the nose with a pencil (or you can stick in cloves). Now you have a toothpick porcupine!"

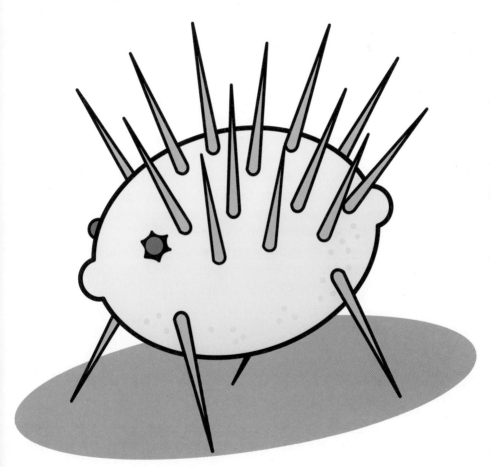

Names

A name is special.

I know you by name.

~ Exodus 33:17

What's in a Name?

Mary and Jack loved to go to the doctor's office because after they saw the doctor, the nurse let each of them choose a lollipop. That was the best part of the visit!

One day when Mary and Jack went to the doctor, he asked Mary, "What's your name?"

"I'm Baby," Mary answered.

"How old are you?" asked the doctor.

When Mary didn't answer right away, Jack said, "She's two."

"No I'm not!" Mary said, "I'm Baby!"

Mary liked to be called "Baby" because it had special meaning to her. She didn't know the meaning behind "Mary" yet, so "Baby" was more important to her.

Most parents name their kids for special reasons. Some parents choose names just because they sound nice, but a lot of parents pick a name because it means something. For example, you might be named after your grandma or a Bible character or a special friend of your family's.

In the same way, God's name is very special. When you hear the name "God" you know that He is your God and your friend. Be sure to always say the names "God" or "Jesus" only in nice ways.

Your Turn

1. What name did Mary want to be called? Why?

_____

_____

2. Do you know what your name means? Why did your parents pick that name?

_____

_____

Prayer

I'm glad You have such a nice name, God. Thank You for parents who gave me a special name, too. Amen.

Names

Read this to your child: "When you hear God's name you know who He is because His name is special. Here are some other things that have names. Point to each one and think of at least three names for each. Now go look in a mirror. Who is that person called? Why is she called by that name? Does she have more than one name? How many?"

Payment

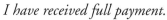

Only God's love is free.

I have received full payment.

~ Philippians 4:18

The Mommy Tax

"Here you go," said Mommy to Regina as she handed her some cheese sticks. "Thank you," Regina said, "but why is there one missing from the package?"

"Oh that's because of the mommy tax," answered Mommy.

"What's the mommy tax?" asked Regina.

Mommy smiled and said, "That means because I bought the cheese sticks from the store and opened them up for you, I get to have one as payment."

Regina thought about what Mommy said. "I guess that's fair," she decided.

From then on, when Mommy bought a treat for Regina, Regina would always give Mommy a little taste. She was paying the "mommy tax."

Regina had to pay something for her treats, even if it was just for fun. That's the way it is with most things in life. There's only one thing that is truly free, and that's God's love for you. You don't have to pay anything for His love!

Your Turn

1. Why did Mommy take one of the cheese sticks?

_____

_____

2. Can you think of some things that you or your parents have to pay for?

_____

_____

Prayer

Thank You, God, for loving me for free. Amen.

Envelope Car

Read this to your child: "Most things in life have to be paid for in some way. The only thing that is really free is love. God loves you no matter what—and there's no tax on love. The cheese sticks that Mommy bought for Regina didn't cost much, but some things do cost a lot. One thing that costs a lot of money is a car. You can make your own car in a way that doesn't cost much at all! Just draw a picture on the side of an envelope (as shown below). Make sure that the top of the car is on the connected part of the envelope. Lick the envelope and seal it. Now cut out your car (careful not to cut the top). Color your car, and then spread it open. Vroom, vroom, drive away!"

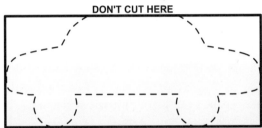

Death

I will live forever because Jesus
already died for me.

Whoever…believes in me will never die.

~ John 11:26

Pulling Plants

"You'll have to pull some of the plants out," said Mommy as she looked at Jordan's planter full of small, green seedlings. Jordan had planted a handful of parsley and basil seeds in the pot of dirt, and now they were about an inch tall.

"No," cried Jordan. "I don't want to pull any of them out. They'll die."

"But if you don't pull them out," said Mommy, "then all of them will die. There isn't enough room for them all to grow."

"I don't want the plants to die," Jordan said sadly. "Why can't they all live?"

"If people never died," said Mommy, "and more and more babies kept being born, we would run out of food and houses and everything!

"Yeah, I guess so," Jordan answered.

"Well, the plants are the same way," said Mommy. "Unless some of them are pulled out, there won't be enough dirt and food for them. They will all die. But if we pull out some of the plants, then the rest will grow."

Jordan learned that death is a part of life. Only through the death of some plants were the others able to live. If all the plants had been left in the dirt, none of them would have survived. In the same way, if Jesus hadn't died for you on the cross, you wouldn't be able to survive. Because He faced death for you, you will live.

Your Turn

1. Why did Jordan need to pull out some of the plants?

_____

_____

2. Who died so you could live?

_____

_____

Prayer

Jesus, thank You for dying on the cross, and rising again, so that I could live. Amen.

Seedlings

Read this to your child: "Jesus died on the cross so that you could live. You can start a pot of plants just like Jordan did, but don't forget to pull some of them out once they get about an inch tall. Find a small dish (an empty butter or whipped topping dish works well). Place a shallow layer of gravel over the bottom of the dish, and then fill with potting soil. Plant some seeds (herb seeds, such as parsley, work well) and water. Place the dish in the sun and wait. Once the plants are about an inch tall, pull some out so there's plenty of room for the others to grow. The great part about using herb seeds is that you can eat them once they're all grown up!"

Environment

I should help to keep
God's world clean and beautiful.

God…put him in the Garden of Eden to…take care of it.
~ Genesis 2:15

Chloe's Job

Chloe looked at the containers of motor oil on the garage shelves. Daddy had said it was her job to put them in the back of the truck, but that seemed like a lot of work.

"Why can't we just pour the oil down the drain?" she asked.

"Because that would be bad for the environment," said Daddy.

"But we put dirty water down the drain," Chloe said. "Isn't that bad for the environment, too?"

"No," answered Daddy, "that's not the same thing. Dirty water isn't like oil. Oil would hurt the environment."

"Then let's just put the containers in the garbage can for the garbage man to take away," said Chloe.

"No, we can't do that either," said Daddy. "Oil has to go to a certain place for it to be thrown away. That's why we'll put it in the truck and then I'll take it to that place."

God gave you a beautiful world to live in, and you should try to keep it that way. He wants you to keep His world clean and beautiful.

Your Turn

1. Why couldn't the oil be poured down the drain?

_____

_____

2. How do you help to take care of God's world?

_____

_____

Prayer

Thank You, God, for giving me such a beautiful world to live in. Amen.

 # Beautiful World

Read this to your child: "God wants you to take good care of His world. Here's a picture of the beautiful world for you to finish coloring."

Colors

God created colors.

I, the Lord, have created it.

~ Isaiah 45:8

The Meanings of Colors

"How did the color red come to mean stop?" Lily asked one day in the car. She was looking at a stoplight.

"I'm not sure," Mommy answered. "Maybe it's because people think of the color red as also meaning 'danger' sometimes."

"But why does it sometimes mean danger?" Lily asked.

Mommy thought about that. "Well, I don't know," she finally said. "I guess it might have to do with the fact that the color red sometimes means danger in nature, too."

"What do you mean?" Lily wondered.

"One example is that some insects have red on them to scare birds away from eating them," said Mommy.

Did you ever wonder why some colors, like red, are used to mean "danger" or "stop"? God carefully chose the colors in His world. He decided what those colors should mean in nature, and we've simply followed His example in other things. It is always right to follow God.

Your Turn

1. Can you think of other colors that are used to mean something?

_____

_____

2. What is your favorite color?

_____

_____

Prayer

Thank You, God, for all the beautiful colors in Your world. Amen.

Floating Colors

Read this to your child: "God uses color in nature. You can use His example for a fun activity that uses color. Set out two glasses. Fill each half-full with water. In one glass, add lots of salt. In the other glass, add some food coloring. Now pour the colored water onto the salt water. The salt water is heavier, so the colored water will, for the most part, remain on top (at least for a while). You can experiment with different amounts of salt to see which works best or lasts longer."

I Can Care for Myself

Safety

God wants me to be careful.

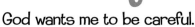

You alone, O Lord, make me dwell in safety.
~ Psalm 4:8

Snow Picnic

"Can Courtney and I have a picnic?" Olivia asked. She had just gotten home from school and was eager to play with her little sister. Mommy was surprised by Olivia's question because it was cold outside.

"I suppose it's okay," said Mommy, "as long as you bundle up and sit on the front porch."

Olivia was excited! She quickly gathered a small basket of jelly beans, pulled on her coat and mittens, and ran outside. Courtney soon followed.

Olivia and Courtney happily sat on the front porch step eating their jelly beans and watching the snow all around them. They were having so much fun that Olivia forgot to watch little Courtney. Suddenly, Mommy heard Olivia running inside crying.

"Courtney stuck a jelly bean up her nose," she yelled. As Courtney walked in, Mommy could see that Courtney's nose had the color orange on it.

It took some time for Mommy to clean all of the jelly bean out of Courtney's nose. Mommy was angry with Olivia and Courtney.

Courtney never should have put a jelly bean in her nose. Instead of just having an orange nose, Courtney could have been hurt. What Courtney did was dangerous. God doesn't want you to do dangerous things. God wants you to be careful so you can stay safe, healthy and happy.

Your Turn

1. Can you remember a time when you did something that was dangerous?

_____

_____

2. Why does God want you to be careful?

_____

_____

Prayer

Dear God, please help me to remember that no matter how much fun I'm having, I still need to be careful and not do dangerous things. Amen.

Pretty Picnic

Read this to your child: "Courtney wasn't very careful at her picnic, so she got all messy and could have even been hurt. Here is a way for you to have a safe picnic at home. Gather together a blanket and some food that you can eat with your fingers without making a mess. Pictures of foods you might like are below. Which ones are neat to eat, and with which ones would you use a fork or spoon? Draw a line from the messy foods to the spoon or knife, and connect the finger foods to the hand."

Growth

God makes me grow stronger every day.

From him the whole body...grows and builds itself up in love.

~ Ephesians 4:16

Mommy Hair

"Fuzzy, fuzzy," cried baby Emma as she stuck out her finger to show Mommy.

"Okay," said Mommy, "bring it here and I'll throw the fuzzy away." Baby Emma carefully held up her hand as Mommy bent forward to see what she had found.

"Why, this isn't a fuzzy at all," said Mommy. "This is a hair."

"Baby hair?" asked Emma.

"No," answered Mommy. "It's a long, blonde Mommy hair. You can just throw it away in the waste basket."

Baby Emma looked down at the hair stuck to her finger and suddenly looked very sad. "Mommy, you're supposed to fix it! Put the hair back on your head!" she cried.

Mommy snuggled Emma close and explained, "Just like you're getting bigger every day, my hair grows, too. You don't need to be sad. We lose hair, but we grow more hair, too."

God made your body so that it is always growing some way. When you're little you grow bigger and bigger every day. Even after you're grown up, you still keep getting smarter and stronger. God made us all that way.

Your Turn

1. Why was Emma sad?

_____

_____

2. Who made your body?

_____

_____

Prayer

Thank You, God, for giving me such a wonderful body that grows and grows. Amen.

What Grows?

Read this to your child: "God made a whole world full of things that grow. Below are some pictures of things that grow, and some things that don't. Can you circle the ones that grow?"

Health

God wants me to take care of my health.

This will bring health to your body and nourishment to your bones.

~ Proverbs 3:8

Bodies Need Good Things

"Kids need a lot of calcium for strong bones," said Lydia. She had been looking at a cartoon on the back of her cereal box. It showed all the things our bodies need to be healthy.

"That's true," answered Mommy. "Kids do need a lot of calcium. That's why it's important that you eat things like milk, cheese and yogurt because they have lots of calcium in them."

"What else do kids need?" asked Lydia.

"Well," said Mommy, "not only kids, but all of us need to eat lots of fruit and vegetables. We all need to make sure that our bodies get the things that they need to be healthy. Vitamins help, too."

God gave you a beautiful and strong body, but you must take good care of your body to keep it that way. God wants you to give your body what it needs so that you can grow big and strong. If you make sure you eat the right things, such as milk and vegetables, you will keep your body healthy. And that shows God you appreciate what He has given you!

Your Turn

1. Why should you eat good things?

_____

_____

2. What does a healthy body show God?

_____

_____

Prayer

Thank You, God, for giving me a wonderful body. Please help me to always take good care of my body so that I can be healthy and strong. Amen.

Helicopters Need Air

Read this to your child: "Everything needs something or someone. God made you in very special ways. Your body needs good food to live. Just like that, helicopters need air to fly. Here's a helicopter you can make yourself. Fly it around the house. What would the helicopter do if there wasn't any air to move its propellers? What would your body do if it didn't have good food and calcium?"

What You Need

cardboard
scissors
paper clip

What to Do

1. Cut and fold a piece of cardboard as shown in the diagram below.

2. Fold one of the strips forward and the other backward.

3. Attach the paper clip at the bottom of the "helicopter."

4. Hold the helicopter high in the air and let it go. Watch it spin its way to the floor!

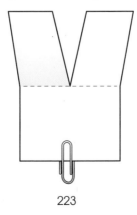

Independence

God wants me to try my best.

Come on, all of you, try again!

~ Job 17:10

Oh My!

"Oh, my!" said Mommy as she walked into the house. Mommy had come home early from work to find Madeline sitting in her high chair, covered with food. There was jelly on her face, peaches in her hair and peanut butter smeared all over her pink shirt.

"What happened here?" Mommy asked Grandma, who had been babysitting.

When Grandma saw Mommy, she was surprised. "I didn't know you'd be home this soon," said Grandma. "I would have had her all cleaned up before you got home. I decided to let Madeline try to feed herself for the first time. She did a pretty good job!"

Grandma knew that it was important for Madeline to learn to do things for herself, even if she made a big mess. Sometimes we don't do things perfectly the first time, but God wants us to try our best. Someday you'll be able to do most things all by yourself. When you are able to do things by yourself, God wants you to help other people learn, too.

Your Turn

1. Why did Grandma think it was important for Madeline to feed herself?

_____

_____

2. What can you do all by yourself?

_____

_____

Prayer

God, please help me to keep trying to do more and more things by myself. Amen.

Fun Fan

Read this to your child: "It could take Madeline a long time to learn to eat by herself, but the only way she could do it is to keep trying. It's okay if you cannot do things well right away. God just wants you to try your best. Here's a project that may take you a little practice before you get it right, but in no time at all, you'll learn to do it if you don't give up. Take a piece of paper and color it any way you like. Then fold the paper into strips, first folding one way, and then the opposite. When the paper is all folded, hold one end in your hand and spread out the folds. Now you have a pretty fan!"

Caution

God wants me to use caution before I act.

A fool is…reckless.

~ Proverbs 14:16

Chicken Surprise

"Go back!" laughed Jessica as she ran as fast as she could after the brown and white chicken. The chicken had flown out of the coop. It was eating the corn out of the garden when Jessica saw it.

"Get out of my garden!" she hollered as she chased it across the yard.

Suddenly the chicken stopped and turned around. Jessica was so busy chasing the chicken that she didn't consider it might decide to chase her. As the chicken started toward her, Jessica was surprised and afraid. Even though she had just been laughing, she was now screaming as she ran as fast as she could toward the house. The chicken chased her the whole way!

Sometimes you think you understand how things are, but then they change. What looks safe at first can turn out to be not so safe. The chicken looked like fun to chase, but Jessica soon learned that wasn't true. You should think carefully about what you choose to do before you do it, so that you're not surprised by how it all turns out.

The life that God gave you is very important and special. That's why you should always be very careful to think before you do something so you do not get hurt.

Your Turn

1. Why do you think the chicken chased Jessica?

_____

_____

2. Why should you be careful to think before you act?

_____

_____

Prayer

Dear God, please help me to remember that I should think carefully about what I choose to do before I do it. Amen.

Flying Butterfly

Read this to your child: "God wants you to think carefully about what you do before you do it. Here's something for you to think about carefully if you want it to turn out correctly. Fold a piece of paper in half. Draw a pattern on it like the one shown below. Now cut on the line–but not on the fold!–and open it. It's a butterfly! If you punch a hole in the center, you can stick your finger through and make the butterfly fly. You can even color the butterfly to make it extra pretty."

Adulthood

I should do more for God as I grow older.

I made you grow like a plant of the field.
~ Ezekiel 16:7

Growing Up

"Let me get it, let me get it," hollered Oscar. Mommy had just seen a big, black spider on the wall. She was running to get a tissue so she could catch it. She was surprised to hear that Oscar wanted to do it.

"Why do you want to get it?" asked Mommy.

"Let me get the spider," answered Oscar, "because then I'm a man!"

"I want to be grown up, too," said Oscar's sister, Wendy, "so let me do it. I want to be a woman."

Mommy shook her head at both of them. "Getting a bug off the wall doesn't mean that you're all grown up," explained Mommy. "Besides, there are some people who are all grown up but are still afraid of bugs. That doesn't mean that they're not adults."

Being grown up isn't just about catching bugs or staying up late. There's a lot more to it than that! When you grow up you will be smarter, stronger and able to help those who are younger than you are. As God helps you to grow into an adult, He will want you to teach those younger than you about Him and the Bible. You can do many things for God now, but you will be able to do even more as you grow older.

Your Turn

1. What kinds of things will you be able to do when you're an adult?

_____

_____

2. What kinds of things can you do for God now?

_____

_____

Prayer

God, please help me to remember I can do many things for You at my age now. I want to grow into an adult who serves You. Amen.

Adult or Child

Read this to your child: "God made you able to do certain things when you're little, and certain things when you're grown up, but there's more to being an adult than just what you can or can't do. God expects a lot of you as you grow older. Can you tell the difference between things that adults can do and things children can do? Look at the pictures below. Draw a line from the girl to the things that she can do, then connect the adult to the things that she can do. Finish coloring the pictures when you're done."

Discipline

God wants me to have discipline.

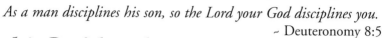

As a man disciplines his son, so the Lord your God disciplines you.
~ Deuteronomy 8:5

Yolanda's Punishment

"To the corner," said Mommy as she pointed her finger. "Right now!"

Yolanda had just dumped a dozen eggs onto the floor in front of the refrigerator. Mommy had told Yolanda to stay out of the refrigerator because it was very full, but Yolanda opened the door anyway. The eggs fell out onto the floor. Now Mommy had to punish Yolanda.

"No!" Yolanda screamed as the tears ran down her face. "No, no, no!"

"Go," said Mommy again as she started to count, "one…two…three…."

By the count of three, Yolanda had run to the corner and sat down.

Yolanda had to stay in the corner for four whole minutes because of what she had done. Then Mommy hugged her and talked to her about why she had been punished. Yolanda understood, but she still didn't like that she had to sit in the corner.

Being punished may not feel like a lot of fun, but it is good for you. Punishment helps you learn how to be a good person–a person who has discipline. God wants you to have discipline because that means you know to do right things instead of wrong ones.

Your Turn

1. Is punishment a good thing or a bad thing?

_____

_____

2. Why does God want you to have discipline?

_____

_____

Prayer

Thank You, God, for giving me parents who love me enough to punish me sometimes. Amen.

Counting Eggs

Read this to your child: "Punishment helps you to be a better person. When you are punished, you learn discipline. God wants you to be a person with discipline. Yolanda disobeyed her mommy and dumped eggs on the floor. She not only made a big mess, she wasted good eggs. Some pictures of eggs are below. Can you count how many are in each picture? Color the correct number of eggs for each carton."

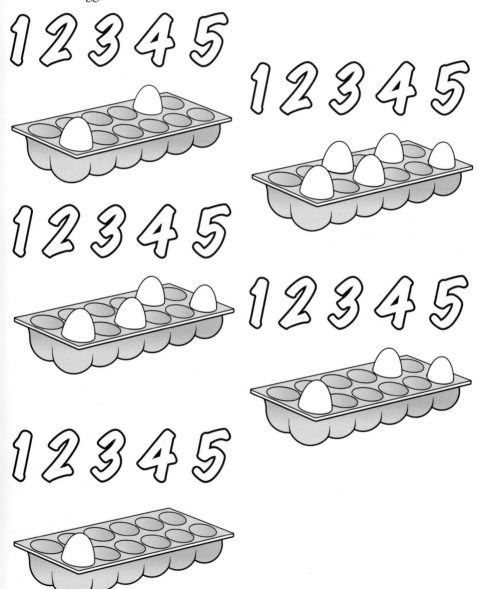

Illness

God helps me when I am sick.

The Lord will...restore him from his bed of illness.

~ Psalm 41:3

I Feel Better!

Grace thumped down the stairs, happy that it was finally morning. She hadn't slept very well, and she was glad to come downstairs and get dressed for the day. The first thing she wanted to do was find Mommy.

"Good morning, Grace," said Mommy as she saw Grace come around the corner.

"I puked," Grace said.

"What?" Mommy asked, hoping that she had heard wrong.

"I puked!" Grace cried again. "My bed's a mess!"

Mommy felt Grace's forehead. She didn't have a fever. In fact, in every other way she seemed fine.

"Well, you seem okay now," said Mommy. "It must have been just a very quick sickness."

"After I got sick I prayed to God that I would feel better," said Grace. "Then I fell asleep and when I woke up I did feel better!"

Illness is a part of life. Sometimes you will get sick, as Grace did, but you can pray and ask God to help you feel better. Sometimes people do stay sick or get worse, but usually people get better like Grace did. Either way, God will always be there for you.

Your Turn

1. What did Grace do after she got sick?

_____

_____

2. Can you remember the last time you were sick? What happened?

_____

_____

Prayer

Dear God, I know that sometimes I will get sick, but thank You for taking care of me and helping me to feel better. Amen.

Healthy Grace

Read this to your child: "Everybody gets sick sometimes. That's just a part of life. But even when you're sick, God is with you, helping you feel better. Here's a picture of Grace playing now that she feels better (turn it sideways to see it correctly). You can finish coloring it."

Bodies

God makes each body different.

I am...wonderfully made.

~ Psalm 139:14

Agreeing with Onions

"My tummy hurts," said Marissa.

"I knew you shouldn't have eaten those onions," Mommy said. "They never seem to agree with you."

"What do you mean?" asked Marissa.

Mommy explained, "Your body just doesn't like onions very much."

"But your body likes onions," Marissa pointed out. "Quentin's body likes onions too. So why doesn't mine?"

"I'm not sure," answered Mommy. "All of our bodies are different. My tummy hurts when I eat sausage, but yours doesn't."

"What about Daddy?" Marissa asked, trying to remember when she'd last seen him eat onions. "Does Daddy's body agree with onions?"

Mommy laughed. "Well, most of the time it does," she said. "It just depends how many he eats."

All bodies work in slightly different ways. That is because God made each person special. No one has a body exactly like another person.

Your Turn

1. Is there something that your body doesn't "agree" with?

_____

_____

2. Who made all bodies different?

_____

_____

Prayer

God, thank You for making me like other people in some ways, but different in my own special ways. Amen.

Everyone Is Different

Read this to your child: "God made each person different and special. A picture of Marissa is below. Think of all the ways that you can make her different from how you look. Color her hair, clothes and everything else to be different from you."

Hygiene

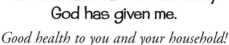

I should take care of the body God has given me.

Good health to you and your household!

~ 1 Samuel 25:6

Tiny Pearls

Sabrina loved to brush her teeth. Mommy helped Sabrina brush her teeth in the morning, but every night Sabrina got to do it by herself.

Sabrina knew it was very important to take good care of her teeth so they stayed healthy. She loved being the one to take care of them at night.

Sabrina had a pretty pink toothbrush with a picture of a princess on it. Each night she would carefully squeeze a tiny bit of toothpaste onto it before gently brushing it back and forth across her teeth. She would brush and brush until all of her teeth were clean.

One day as Grandma was visiting, Grandma said "My, how beautiful your teeth are, Sabrina. They're so white and shiny, they're like tiny pearls."

From that day forward, Sabrina's always called her teeth "tiny pearls."

Sabrina took good care of her teeth. God wants you to take care of your body. He only gives you one, so you must keep it healthy.

Your Turn

1. What did Grandma call Sabrina's teeth?

_____

_____

2. Why does God want you to take care of your body?

_____

_____

Prayer

God, thank You for giving me a body. I'll try my best to keep it healthy. Amen.

Healthy Activities

Read this to your child: "God wants you to take good care of your body so it stays healthy. Sabrina took good care of her teeth, but there are many other things you can do to keep your body healthy. Circle the pictures below that show how to keep a body healthy."

Protection

God protects me in many ways.

He has given us...protection.

~ Ezra 9:9

Taking Care of Kayla

Kayla saw Mommy putting on her coat and shoes.

"Where are you going?" Kayla asked.

"It's okay," answered Mommy. "I'm just taking your sister to school."

"But who will take care of me?" Kayla cried.

"Don't worry," said Mommy. "Daddy is still here. He'll wait until I get back before he leaves for work."

After Mommy left, Kayla watched as Daddy got dressed for work. "What if Mommy doesn't get back before you leave?" asked Kayla. "Who will take care of me then?"

Daddy gave Kayla a quick hug and said, "Don't worry. I'll wait until she gets back. Besides, you never have to worry. There will always be someone to take care of you. If Mommy or I weren't here, then Grandma and Grandpa would take care of you."

"What if they couldn't take care of me?" asked Kayla.

"Then Aunt Jennifer or Uncle Pete would watch over you," answered Daddy. "You never need to worry. God is always with you, too. There will always be someone to protect and care for you, no matter what."

God protects you in many ways. He sent Jesus to protect you from your sins. He gave you parents to care for you and keep you safe, and He watches over you all the time, no matter where you are or what you are doing.

Your Turn

1. Who did Daddy say would take care of Kayla?

_____

_____

2. Who will always take care of you?

_____

_____

Prayer

Thank You, God, for always protecting and caring for me. Amen.

Ways of Protection

Read this to your child: "God protects you in many different ways. The pictures below show a few of the ways God protects you. Discuss each of them with your mommy or daddy. Can you think of another way that you are protected? Draw a picture of it at the bottom of the page. When you're all done with your picture, you can finish coloring the others."